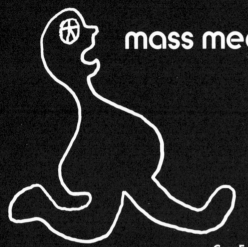

mass media / a worktext in the processes of modern communication

by Ann Christine Heintz, B.V.M.

M. Lawrence Reuter, S.J.

and Elizabeth Conley

ComEd Series Director   George Lane, S.J.

Loyola University Press   Chicago, Illinois   60657

Communication Education

Editing   George Lane, S.J.

Design   Catherine Connelly

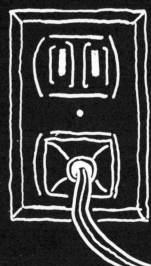

The authors and Loyola University Press are deeply grateful to the teachers, students, newsmen, and publishers who contributed to this book. All formal acknowledgments are listed on pages 239-40.

contents

Introduction   4
Media Ecology   7

INTERACTION:

THE MEDIA AND THE PEOPLE   19

The People's Choice

Qualities of Popular Taste   21
Audience Thresholds   27
Individual Tastes   33
Measuring Popular Taste   38
Special Tastes and
        Special Audiences   44

The Decision Makers

Media Men and
        Their Audiences   57
Advertisers and Consumers   68
The TV Rating Game   78

The Media Image and Massage

TV and Behavior   89
Media and Culture   97

THE NEWS MEDIA   107

The People's Need to Know

Quality of Knowledge
        and Quality of Life   109
Personal News Inventory   114

The Professional Newsman

Straight News Reporting   121
Interpretative Reporting   126
"Made News"   133
Investigative Reporting   139
Involvement Reporting   145

Critique of the News

Instant News   151
The Newsman's
        Specialized Knowledge   158
Quality News Sources   163
Stock Reporting   170
The Newsman and
        His Sources   174

Editing and Ownership

The News Relay Process   181
The Gatekeeper Process   188
The Gatekeepers' Power   196
Ownership and News   202

MASS MEDIA

IN A DEMOCRATIC SOCIETY   211

The People's Right to Know

Classification
        of Information   213
Censorship   219

Feedback and Feed-in

Talking Back to the Media   227
Media Access   232

Acknowledgments   239

introduction

The ComEd program is based on the assumption that young people are profoundly influenced and in fact educated by the mass media. It makes an effort, then, to open out the classroom walls, or to bring the media environment in to create a global classroom, a place where TV, films, radio, newspapers, magazines, and all types of advertising can be examined, analyzed, understood, critically judged, and evaluated.

It is obvious that the worktext is only a key to the program, a starting point and a guide. The success of this course, more than others, depends on student involvement and initiative. The primary material of the course is the general media experience of each student, what he has seen, heard, and experienced in his everyday life.

MASS MEDIA—A STUDY IN PROCESS

There's something stable and enduring about the poetry of Robert Browning and the novels of John Steinbeck. There's something very unstable and fleeting about the mass media. The media themselves change and develop. The formats of media packages change. The needs and interests of audiences change. And so, because they are so much in process, it would be foolish to try to study the mass media the way we've traditionally studied other literature. We propose, instead, to study the mass media the way scientists study other things that are constantly changing.

First, the scientist must pose the right question and specify his inquiry so that he has a clearly defined area for experimenting and collecting data. During this course we will call this leading question a Probe. A social scientist might ask a question about crowd behavior. A communications scientist, which you will be throughout this course, might ask a question about the effect of violence on TV or the effect of the news media on democratic elections.

4

LAB

Once the question has been raised and specified, the scientist sets up a laboratory procedure. Each Lab in this worktext calls for careful, controlled execution, just as a physics or chemistry experiment does. The Lab provides the experience input. It aims to bring the media world into the classroom, to help you learn by simulating the actual problems and processes of the print and electronic media. As you work through each Lab, you must carefully observe what happens and accurately record the data.

FOCUS

When the data has been collected and recorded, the scientist asks a new set of questions. What does the experiment prove? What relationships emerge? Are there any clear patterns in the process that repeat themselves? What does the evidence really mean? Focus questions like these come after every Lab. They are only starters. If you are a curious scientist, you will have many more questions of your own. Challenge your conclusions, ask others to support theirs, and be willing to admit the limitations of your findings.

INTERFACE

Interface is a confrontation between an individual and some aspect of his environment. The Lab exercises mainly deal with the problems and processes of the professional media. But similar problems, processes, and experiences can be found in your own life at school and home. For instance, after you ask how media men understand their audiences, you can also ask how teachers understand their audiences. The Interface questions explore your own experiences, feelings, and values.

We do not ordinarily think of school as a mass medium of communication, but there is a real sense in which it is, and the Interface does approach it that way. You may be personally involved in the same problems at school as the print and broadcast men are in their work. Interface brings the study closer to home for a more dynamic realization of the experience and emotions involved.

INVESTIGATE

The Investigate section of each unit proposes spin-offs from the main thrust of the Lab. There are suggestions for history buffs and technical types, for creative artists and curious researchers. Space in the book is limited; spin-offs for further investigation are limitless. We only offer a few starters. Hopefully, you will come up with many additional inquiries.

Where I Stand -

Each major unit in MASS MEDIA contains a Where I Stand-- exercise, a challenge for you to determine what your personal position is on a main issue in the unit.

SIMULATE

"Where I Stand--" is immediately followed by Simulate, a brief exercise, once you have taken a stand, to help you realize how your position might work out in practice.

. . . And the process goes on. We hope through this course you will grow as critical thinkers. We hope the course will help you develop your sense of responsibility and involvement in the future evolution of the mass media. We hope you will become a creative force in bringing about that evolution. And especially, we hope you will enjoy the course even when it makes serious demands of you.

The Authors

Media Ecology

The investigations set out in this book are
largely concerned with the mass media
as "mass message."

But there is another whole area of investigation concerned with how the media
rub against our senses creating a new
environment for us. This area can be
called media ecology because it deals
with the relationship between living orga-
nisms, like men, and the physical realities of the media, like sound waves,
light waves, and electronics. Media
ecology asks how instant speed reshapes
information space and time. Such investigations could easily fill a book by themselves; we cannot begin to treat them
adequately in the introduction to this one.

And yet, any investigation of the mass
media and its influence on modern man
would be seriously weakened if the investigator did not have at least some ac-
quaintance with the general areas of
media ecology. To provide this acquaint-
ance we are going to propose a sampling
of statements about these ecological hap-
penings. The statements are divided into
ten sections which relate closely to the
rest of the book. We suggest that you consider each of the quotations, discuss them
with the class, challenge and debate them,
and then, if possible, pursue the inquiry
further with specialists in the physical,
biological, and behavioral sciences. Once
you have examined and evaluated the statements, they will provide a context for approaching the main exercises in the book.

THE SOUND ENVIRONMENT

Today we immerse ourselves in sound. We've all become acoustic skindivers. Music is no longer for listening to, but for merging with.

EDMUND CARPENTER

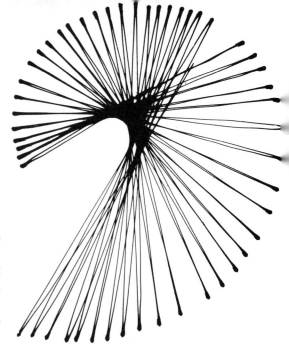

At a given instant I hear not merely what is in front of me or behind me or at either side, but all these things simultaneously, and what is above and below as well. . . . I not only can but must hear all the sounds around me at once. Sound thus situates me in the midst of a world.

WALTER ONG

Generally speaking, radio functions as a diverting "companion," and it helps to fill voids that are created by (1) routine and boring tasks and (2) feelings of social isolation and loneliness.

HAROLD MENDELSOHN

The greater reality of words and sound is seen also in the further paradox that sound conveys meaning more powerfully and accurately than sight.

WALTER ONG

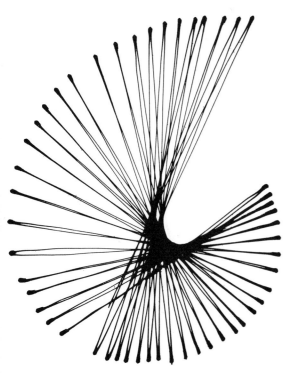

Contemporary popular songs and modern music are generally much more sensuous than intellectual or spiritual experiences. Modern music has a visceral quality: when a singer like Tom Jones takes the microphone, no one remains indifferent. . . . The whole audience gets involved in the act.

PIERRE BABIN

The rock sound overwhelms separateness, the mental operations that discern and define here and there, me and not-me are pounded by volume, riddled by light; the listener slides free from the restraining self and from the pretenses of a private, "unique" rationality.

BENJAMIN DE MOTT

Sound unites groups of living beings as nothing else does.

WALTER ONG

Sight is swift, comprehensive, simultaneously analytic and synthetic. It requires so little energy to function, as it does, at the speed of light, that it permits our minds to receive and hold an infinite number of items of information in a fraction of a second. With sight, infinities are given at once; wealth is its description.   CALEB GATTEGNO

The sense of sight operates through the formation of visual concepts, that is, through shape patterns, which are fitted to the appearance of objects in the environment.

RUDOLPH ARNHEIM

When we listen to speech, we need to wait until the end of each sentence to understand what is meant; while the act of looking at a landscape provides immediate and simultaneous information from an infinite number of sources.   CALEB GATTEGNO

There is a curious paradox about a picture—it is neither a pure display on the one hand nor a pure deception on the other. The stimulus conveys information for both what it is physically and what it stands for.   JAMES J. GIBSON

Eyes normally take in chunks of reality.   CALEB GATTEGNO

A work of visual art, in other words, is not an illustration of the thoughts of its maker, but rather the final manifestation of that thinking itself.   RUDOLPH ARNHEIM

Print created the drive for self-expression, self-portraiture (Montaigne, Rembrandt), but in time it rendered illegible the faces of men. . . . Photography, film, TV, aided us in the recovery of gesture and facial awareness—a language of moods and emotions never adequately expressed in words and totally lost in print.   EDMUND CARPENTER

COEXPRESSION

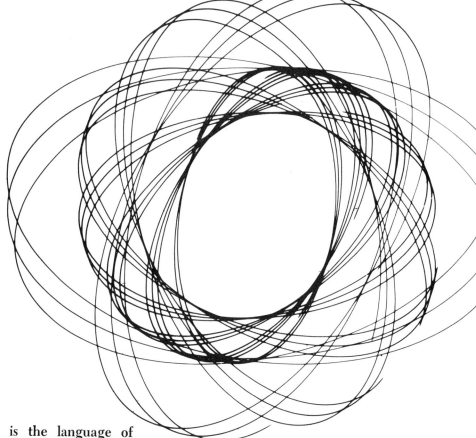

Coexpression, though still young, is the language of twentieth century communications, a language dependent on two senses, two styles, two sensibilities—and creating a new sense of information, a new way of reaching another, a fresh way of thinking.

WILLIAM KUHNS AND ROBERT STANLEY

TV and movies are both watched, but with different effects. Since the whole sensorium seeks participation in all sense activity, the senses directly affected by high definition stimuli [movies] will tend to become passive, and the senses not stimulated [TV] . . . will tend to become active.

JOHN CULKIN

When an image and words can coalesce to form a fresh kind of language—demanding an interplay between words and image, and between the word-image combination and the reader or viewer—then coexpression has happened. The interplay, a key selling factor in many ads or commercials and one of the mainstays of comics, makes coexpression more complex than pure words in its mode of involvement, and hence capable of creating a wider range of responses.

WILLIAM KUHNS AND ROBERT STANLEY

A United States Navy study showed that audience retention is far greater when the viewer is exposed to both sight and sound [television] than when he is exposed to sight [newspapers] or sound [radio] alone.

Coexpression joins the precision of words to the immediate power of images.

WILLIAM KUHNS

10

. . . the environment imposed by print itself: one word after the other, one sentence after another, one paragraph after another, one page after another, one thing at a time in a logical, connected line. The effects of this linear thinking are deep and influence every facet of a literate society such as our own. HOWARD GOSSAGE

If oral communication keeps people together, print is the isolating medium par excellence. DAVID RIESMAN

Many people misunderstand McLuhan when he says that print is dead. Generally they're book-men whose bias makes them impervious to the effects of the medium. They see more and more books being sold and conclude that, despite television, print is still very much alive. This is true.

But, as a psychological environment, print is dead. In other words although print is still around, future generations, imprinted by television will no longer relate to the world through a print-grid or print mentality.

Rather, electronic reality is what's shaping print. Books manifest this in both internal style and form. Staccato anthologies and random access books, especially magazines, are the central print forms, not ponderous and linear developmental novels.

Moreover, you can probably argue that people are reading more because of TV, not despite it. After all, speed-of-light information flow hooks us on data. To feed our habits we need an accelerated information input which print, because of its low cost and high variety and access, can provide. MICHAEL SHAMBERG

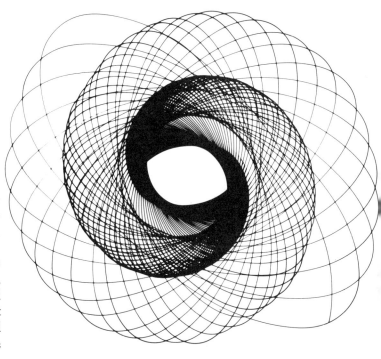

The book, like the door, is an encouragement to isolation: the reader wants to be alone, away from the noise of others. This is true even of comic books for children, who associate comics with being alone, just as they associate TV with the family, and movies with friends of their own age. DAVID RIESMAN

Emotion tends to beget bodily motion. In Homer, the manliest warriors wept openly, beat their chests, tore their hair, and when this was sung about in the Athenian markets, it's probable listeners joined in the expression of these emotions. Hearing these accounts meant experiencing them. But one can read them without emotion. Any newspaper front page is a mass of tragedies, yet we read them unmoved. EDMUND CARPENTER

ELECTRONIC WORLD

As electrically contracted, the globe is no more than a village.
MARSHALL MCLUHAN

A child who gets his environmental training on television —and very few nowadays do not—learns the same way any member of a pre-literate society learns: from the direct experience of his eyes and ears, without Gutenberg for a middle man. Of course they do learn how to read too, but it is a secondary discipline not primary as it is with their elders.
HOWARD GOSSAGE

Electronic media have made all the arts environmental. Everyone can avail himself of cultural riches beyond what any millionaire has ever known.
EDMUND CARPENTER

The images of the electronic world represent a continual flow of data, not measured or measurable. This process has been described as a "mosaic" effect of composite impressions producing a total comprehension. Many effects and impressions are absorbed by the viewer instantaneously, involving fusion of all the senses. The spectator becomes part of the system or process and must supply the connections. He is the screen upon which images are projected.
JOHN JOHANSEN

We're all electric generators. Electronic media outer our senses: they extend the human sensorium. That extension is shared: electronic media join us to a common nervous system. Just as a blind man's cane extends his body, providing information a hand or foot might provide, so electric media extend our senses, to a global scale. Our electronic nerve endings now reach every part of the world and we function as humans acting on sense data provided by these electronic extensions.
EDMUND CARPENTER

Just as the Eskimo has been de-tribalized via print, going in the course of a few years from primitive nomad to literate technician, so we, in an equally brief period, are becoming tribalized via electronic channels.
MARSHALL MCLUHAN

The medium, or process, of our time—electric technology —is reshaping and restructuring patterns of social interdependence and every aspect of our personal life. It is forcing us to reconsider and reevaluate practically every thought, every action, and every institution formerly taken for granted. Everything is changing—you, your family, your neighborhood, your education, your job, your government, your relation to "the others." And they're changing dramatically.
MARSHALL MCLUHAN

With the dawn of the Electric Age, time and speed themselves have become of negligible importance; just flip the switch. Instant speed.   HOWARD GOSSAGE

But the effect of the instant motion, or world travel by tv, is to abolish all previous patterns of time and space divisions. All times and all spaces are here and now in an immediate confrontation.   MARSHALL MCLUHAN

Because television enables us to be there, anywhere, instantly, precisely because it fills the instant present moment with experience so engrossing and overwhelming, it dulls our sense of the past.   DANIEL J. BOORSTIN

Time is given man by life. But to live is to exchange this time for as much experience as it can buy. Television, using simultaneously at least two forms of time . . . is telling man that he may now . . . act upon the transformations and provide perhaps an economy for the exchange of time into experience that will move more and more experience from the present randomness to an understanding that is true to reality.   CALEB GATTEGNO

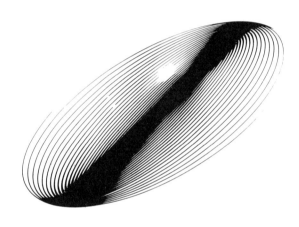

The newspaper world like that of wild beasts exists solely in the present; Press consciousness (if one can speak of consciousness) is circumscribed by simple present time extending from the morning on to the evening edition . . . If you read a paper a week old, . . . no longer is it a newspaper but a memorial.   KAREL CAPEK

Reading and writing are means for converting auditory into visual information and back again, with considerable impoverishment in process. Electronic audio-visual recording, transmission, and reproduction convey information unchanged from its original (save by remaining mechanical infidelity), while immensely lengthening its reach in time and space.   NELSON FOOTE

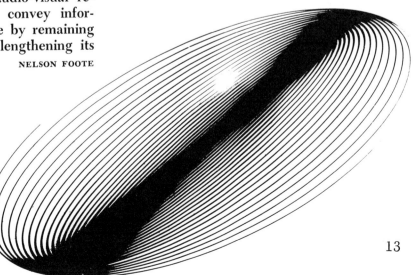

MEDIA AND SPACE

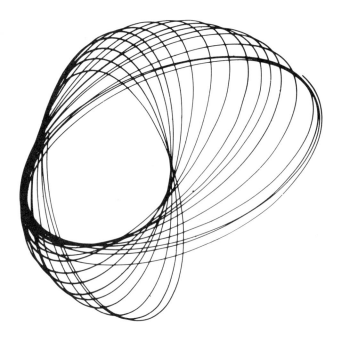

Today the world has shrunk in the wash with speeded-up information movement from all directions. We have come, as it were, to live in a global village. MARSHALL McLUHAN

All man-made material things can be treated as extensions of what man once did with his body or some specialized part of his body. TV, telephones, and books which carry the voice across both time and space are examples of material extensions. EDWARD HALL

Electric circuitry is re-creating in us the multidimensional space orientation of the "primitive." MARSHALL McLUHAN

In Media-America, we are extended in an information-space which is as real psychologically as geographical terrain is physically. In other words, TV cannot be understood as a representation of physical reality. Nor is it an extension of anything. It is its own reality. . . . Television is also a natural resource. Not only does it physically use publicly held space (i.e., airwaves and cables), but the psychological space it inhabits is our collective intelligence. MICHAEL SHAMBERG

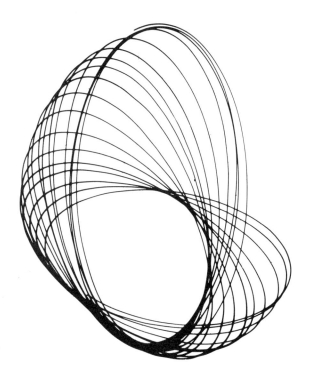

Non-Euclidean space, and the dissolution of our entire Western fabric of perception, results from electric modes of moving information. This revolution involves us willy-nilly in the study of modes and media as forms that shape and reshape our perceptions. MARSHALL McLUHAN

Electronic media have created a global village where all walls between peoples, arts, cultures come tumbling down like the walls of Jericho. EDMUND CARPENTER

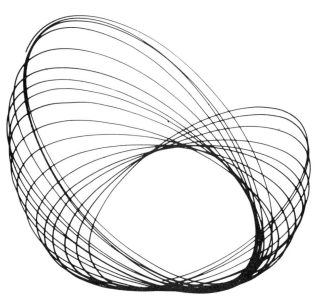

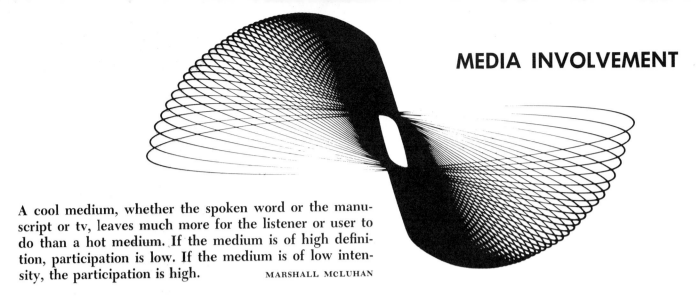

MEDIA INVOLVEMENT

A cool medium, whether the spoken word or the manuscript or tv, leaves much more for the listener or user to do than a hot medium. If the medium is of high definition, participation is low. If the medium is of low intensity, the participation is high.   MARSHALL MCLUHAN

It was the funeral of President Kennedy that most strongly proved the power of television to invest an occasion with the character of corporate participation. It involves an entire population in a ritual process.   MARSHALL MCLUHAN

For audio-visual man, understanding is above all sensitivity to and participation in the rhythm of this world. It is to be "in" and "with," grasping reality not only through intellectual understanding, but through a vital contact with reality itself. Reflection and critical thinking are being increasingly replaced by a need to participate, a yearning for action that can transform or at least better the human condition.   PIERRE BABIN

Literacy and its attendant technology promoted detachment and objectivity, detribalization and individuality. Electric circuitry has the opposite effect: it involves in depth. It merges individual and environment.   EDMUND CARPENTER

In an electric information environment, minority groups can no longer be contained—ignored. Too many people know too much about each other. Our new environment compels commitment and participation. We have become irrevocably involved with, and responsible for, each other.   MARSHALL MCLUHAN

By virtue of the microphone in his hand, an electronic journalist is automatically a participant in any story he covers, particularly in one as volatile and fluctuating as a riot. There is no rewrite man to temper his immediate emotions, no time to reflect before a typewriter upon what he has seen.   JOHN GREGORY DUNNE

As the speed of information increases, the tendency is for politics to move away from representation and delegation of constituents toward immediate involvement of the entire community in the central acts of decision.   MARSHALL MCLUHAN

MEDIA AND LEARNING

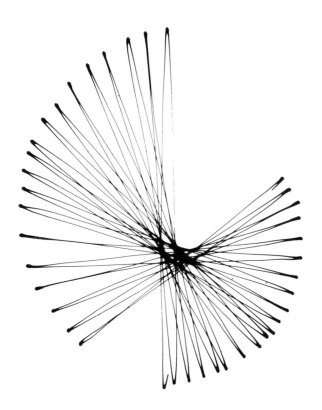

The book is one of the first, and very possibly the most important, mass-produced products, and its impact demonstrates the falsity of the common notion that mass production per se brings about the massification of men.

DAVID RIESMAN

Today in our cities, most learning occurs outside the classroom. The sheer quantity of information conveyed by press-magazines-film-TV-radio far exceeds the quantity of information conveyed by school instruction and texts. This challenge has destroyed the monopoly of the book as a teaching aid and cracked the very walls of the classroom so suddenly that we're confused, baffled.

MARSHALL MCLUHAN

It's misleading to suppose there's any basic difference between education and entertainment.   MARSHALL MCLUHAN

It turns out that TV is a powerful educational medium even when it isn't trying to be, even when it's only trying to entertain. There must be millions of people who have learned, simply by watching crime dramas in the past few years, that they have the right to remain silent when arrested.

HERB SCHLOSSER

Do you in fact think that television stops anybody from reading? Yes, I believe that middle-class children are less well-read than they were, although probably far better informed about public affairs.

KENNETH CLARK

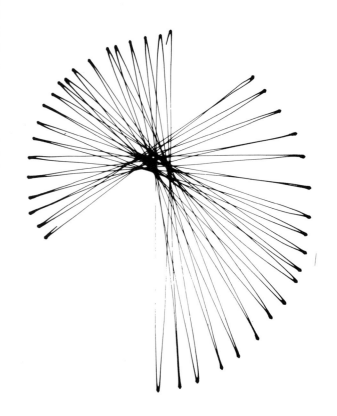

Every minute of television programming—commercials, entertainment, news—teaches us something.

NICHOLAS JOHNSON

By the time a child enters kindergarten he or she has already spent more hours learning about the world in front of the television set than he will spend in a college classroom getting a bachelor's and a master's degree.

ROBERT L. HILLIARD

A great deal of what has been done has been excellent by any standards, and it has vastly increased people's understanding of human nature, literature and even history. Through television we realize that we are all one, all over the world.
KENNETH CLARK

Just as the printing press democratized learning, so the television set has democratized experience.
DANIEL J. BOORSTIN

. . . The networks . . . have often used their power constructively and creatively to awaken the public conscience. . . . The networks made "hunger" and "black lung disease" national issues . . . [and] have done what no other medium could have done in terms of dramatizing the horrors of war. . . . They focus the nation's attention on its environmental abuses . . .
SPIRO AGNEW

Video, by its very nature, is a cultural barbiturate.
JACK GOULD

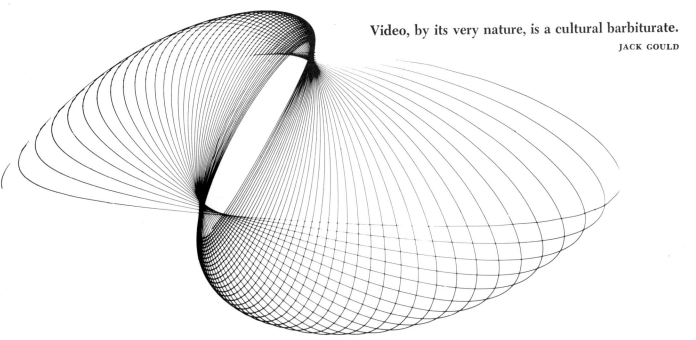

If TV is such a social menace, why are broken sets generally repaired as urgently as leaky plumbing or balky autos?
JACK GOULD

I think you could show bullfights on TV seven nights a week and they'd watch it. They watch TV. TV is painted on the wall. It's part of the family scene.
ROBERT NORTHFIELD, NBC *producer*

Many admirable features of American life today—the new poignance of our conscience, the wondrous universalizing of our experiences, the sharing of the exotic, the remote, the unexpected—come from television. DANIEL J. BOORSTIN

interaction:

the media

& the people

All of us read newspapers, listen to the radio, read magazines, go to movies, and watch television. We have a wide choice of programs and reading, a fantastic variety of information and entertainment lies before us. Never before in the history of man has so much been offered to so many. In the first part of this program we would like to look behind the vast array of media offerings and discover some of the factors that determine what we see and hear. Who makes the decisions; and how do they actually decide what will be printed, what kind of music we'll hear, what programs we'll see, what features we'll read?

There is no single person, no simple formula to answer these questions. Rather, a complex of factors interacting with each other. Three of the most important of these are popular taste, the economics of advertising, and the keen judgment of the decision makers. We'll try to get into each of these and then ask the two large questions: how do the mass media reflect contemporary American society, and then how do they influence that same society?

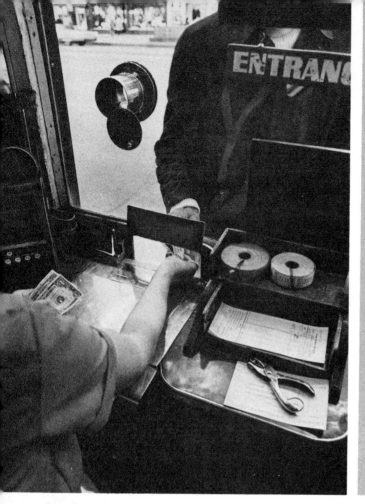

The most striking feature of our contemporary "mass" culture is the vast range and diversity of its alternative cultural choices . . . The "mass," on even cursory examination, breaks down into many different "audiences."

JOHN MCHALE

The old [television] saw the TV audience as a single mass, the means to which was programming for the lowest-common denominator. The new recognized the viewership as several different audiences, and it set out to capture the most desirable, from a commercial standpoint, for itself.

LES BROWN

Today we played a big murder, two accidents, and a society divorce. The UN and the new bond issues got secondary play. We say, "But that is the stuff people are interested in. That's what sells the paper." But is it right?

A MIDWESTERN EDITOR

Certain programs—news, movies, sports and big entertainment specials—can expect to survive and thrive on a mass basis. But the concept of mass programming—reaching the biggest audience with the blandest entertainment—appears to be bankrupt.

LIFE

The People's Choice

While the critics of the mass media march on, vast public audiences continue to buy newspapers and magazines, select movies, and turn the dials of their TV sets. There are literally millions of people picking and choosing every day.

The commentators and critics seldom suggest why the public audiences choose as they do; they seldom identify the qualities of popular taste. Popular taste has to do with feelings, interests, cultural preferences. It is vague and difficult to define, but some of its qualities can be identified.

You are the audience. The following lab is directed at you to see if you can discover some of the qualities of popular taste, some of the preferences that determine why people pick and choose as they do.

 A TASTE TEST

In this lab every student must have an opportunity to create and then to choose the sandwich or the curriculum that he likes best. The better test involves the sense of taste in the sandwich lab, but if food poses problems, an alternate test would involve the creation and choice of an ideal class schedule. Column A proposes the Sandwich Lab; Column B the Curriculum Lab. Follow whichever set of procedures is best suited to your circumstances.

Column A: Sandwich Lab

Hold a Sandwich Bar in class. Every person who can should bring his favorite sandwich to class, a sandwich he really likes. (An alternate approach: set out a wide variety of cold meats, cheeses, breads, condiments, sauces, spreads, lettuce, and tomatoes. Let each person make his own favorite sandwich on the spot.)

Column B: Curriculum Lab

Have the class brainstorm for titles of every possible course offering they can imagine. Start with the course offerings in your school, courses you have heard of in other schools, courses you would like to have offered.

Post or duplicate the list so that each member of the class can then choose any combination of courses he would like to make up the ideal curriculum for himself for this year.

Each member of the class is given a sheet of paper with an assigned number to print out his ideal curriculum.

Display each sandwich, open face, with a number and an evaluation sheet. Keep the maker of each sandwich anonymous. Members of the class should pass along the display and rate each sandwich on its own evaluation sheet (sample below).

Display each curriculum with its number and an evaluation sheet. Keep the curriculum designers anonymous. Members of the class should pass along the display, examine the curricula, and rate each one on its own evaluation sheet.

Sample evaluation sheet:

Check one column to indicate your reaction to this sandwich or this curriculum.
(Sandwich or curriculum number)

# ____	Ideal/ really good	Pretty good	I'm neutral	Unattractive	Awful

MAKE EACH EVALUATION SHEET LARGE ENOUGH TO RECORD the REACTIONS of the whole class.

Each sandwich maker or curriculum designer then totals his own score on his own evaluation sheet. For example,

# 10	Ideal/ really good	Pretty good	I'm neutral	Unattractive	Awful
	X X	X X X X X	X X X X	X X X X X	X
	2	8	8	6	1

He then records his own scores after his own number on a master form on the blackboard or overhead projector.

Master form:

	Ideal/ really good	Pretty good	I'm neutral	Unattractive	Awful
#1					
2					
3					
4					
5					
6					
7					
8					
9					
10					
11					
12					
13					
14					
15					
16					
17					
18					
19					
20					
21					
22					
23					
24					
25					

Column A

Based on the voting recorded on the master form, which sandwich maker would you support to run a sandwich concession in the school cafeteria? Maker of sandwich # ____ .

Now, not before, ask the winning sandwich maker to identify himself and describe his sandwich.

Was the winning sandwich made with cheese? ____ horseradish? ____ tabasco sauce? ____ onions? ____ mayonnaise? ____ garlic? ____ pumpernickel? ____

Column B

Judging from the voting recorded on the master form, which one of the course designers would you support for curriculum director in your school? Designer of curriculum # ____ .

Now, not before, ask the winning curriculum designer to identify himself and describe his ideal curriculum in detail.

Did the winning class schedule include Advanced Greek? ____ Jazz? ____ Black Awareness? ____ English Composition? ____ Math? ____ Guerrilla Theater? ____ Edgar Allan Poe? ____

Judging by the contents of the winning sandwich or class schedule, would you describe it as:

___Unusual   ___Commonplace   ___Complicated   ___Individualistic   ___Bland

Ask the creator of a sandwich which received little or no support to describe his sandwich. Was it made with cheese? ____ horseradish? ____ tabasco sauce? ____ onions? ____ mayonnaise? ____ garlic? ____ pumpernickel? ____

Ask the designer of a class schedule which received little or no support to describe his course choices. Did his schedule include Advanced Greek? ____ Jazz? ____ Black Awareness? ____ English Composition? ____ Math? ____ Guerrilla Theater? ____ Edgar Allan Poe? ____

Judging by the contents of the losing sandwich or class schedule, would you describe it as:

___Unusual   ___Commonplace   ___Complicated   ___Individualistic   ___Bland

Would the winning sandwich be possible for you to make frequently and easily at home?

Would the ideal class schedule be pretty much available in your school right now?

24

Based on the evidence of this lab, draw up a general formula of do's and don'ts for creating products that will have a wide popular taste appeal and will attract the widest possible acceptance.

Formula:

The most popular TV shows of 1969, '70, and '71 are listed below. They represent mass audience tastes in the choice of television programing. Fill in the current top ten shows, then test the formula you devised above against these shows. Do the qualities of popular taste which showed up in the lab also show up in the network television choices?

1969	1970	1971
Wonderful World of Disney	Marcus Welby	Sunday Night at the Movies
Laugh-In	Here's Lucy	All in the Family
Bonanza	Hawaii Five-O	Gunsmoke
Bill Cosby Show	Flip Wilson	Laugh-In
Gunsmoke	Gunsmoke	Marcus Welby
Red Skelton	Ironside	Flip Wilson
My Three Sons	Wonderful World of Disney	Nichols
Here's Lucy	Monday Night Football	Here's Lucy
Family Affair	Bonanza	Cade's County
Mayberry RFD	The FBI	Monday Night Football

Current Top Shows

_____   _____

_____   _____

_____   _____

_____   _____

_____   _____

INTERFACE

Observe the dress and hair styles of the students in your school. What are some of the elements of taste that determine what is popular? What rewards come to those who know and follow what is currently in fashion?

Listen carefully to conversations around your school and neighborhood and at parties. Are there elements of popular taste that determine what topics come up and what things are talked about?

> When I worked on a paper, nothing agitated the readers as much as accidentally leaving out the daily horoscope. The only comparable reaction came from making a typographical error in a recipe on the food page. Nothing printed in the news columns or on the editorial page could compete for impact.
> RICHARD FRISBIE

> TV, like any other business, must make money for stockholders, and the appeal to the lowest common denominator of mass taste is what pays.
> JACK HAMILTON

> Some people say our comics are cheap, and I'm not very fond of them myself. But the devil! Every readership survey has them right up at or near the top readership. They're what the people seem to want. Who am I to censor the public will?
> NEWSPAPER EDITOR

INVESTIGATE

1   ANALYZE a political speech in which a candidate is trying to reach a large number of people. How many specific solutions to specific problems does he offer? How many general proposals? How can you account for this?

2   TRY to find out how or why the word "taste" became associated with people's attraction to different types of literature and arts. Why the metaphor "taste" rather than "sight" or "feel" or "touch"?

3   ATTEMPT to prove that a story line that won great popular acceptance centuries ago can reappear and be popularly accepted in the 1970's much as West Side Story as an adaptation of Romeo and Juliet did in the 1960's.

4   CHOOSE a medium that is generally referred to as a mass audience pleaser of the past, such as the minstrel show, and investigate it carefully to see whether it really met the challenge of satisfying mass audiences.

When your best friend says to you, "You should have seen _____ last night, you really would have liked it," what does he have to know about you, your tastes, and your interests to be right?

Would he suggest "Funky Phantom" or "Johnny Quest"? Or "French Chef" with Julia Childs? Or "Monday Night Football"? Or "Sunday Night at the Movies"--"To Sir With Love"? Or PBL's "Masterpiece Theatre"? Whatever your friend would have suggested, he would also be suggesting that he knows what your're interested in, what you like, what behavioral scientists call your "thresholds." Psychologists tell us that we can best accept new experiences and challenges that lie between our lower and upper thresholds, our readiness area where our interests prepare and motivate us for newness. The experience opportunities that appear too easy or too difficult are less likely to motivate us to respond.

Try the Brain Tease which follows to discover some of your own thresholds. How much energy will you spend to solve a problem? Do your interest areas, do other factors provide added motivation? What effect do your interests have on your media choices?

 **BRAIN TEASE**

Work the following problems sometime in the next twenty-four hours. Do as many as you can. Stay with each one as long as it is a challenge to you.

1   The following string of words doesn't make much sense without the proper punctuation. The challenge is to form these words into a clear sentence by supplying punctuation marks but not changing the position of any word.

It   was   and   I   said   not   are   and   and   and   are   are   not   the   same

2   Make "ergro" into a word by adding three letters in front and three letters in back; the same three letters in the same order.

3   By using four straight lines what is the maximum number of parts into which you can divide the circle?

4   Make a pyramid of a half dollar, a quarter, a nickel, a penny, and a dime in Box B. Now try to make a similar pyramid with the same coins in one of the other boxes. Move the coins one at a time from box to box, but never place a larger coin on top of a smaller one.

A	B	C

5   Begin by placing your pencil on the dot labeled "Begin" in the diagram below. Without lifting the pencil from the paper, draw a continuous line which crosses each line just once, ending at the dot labeled "End."

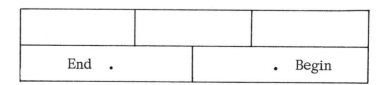

6 Climb the word ladder by changing only one letter per rung, forming a complete word at each rung. For example:

| HATE |
| HAVE |
| HIVE |
| LIVE |
| LOVE |

Now see if you can climb the ladder from SEED to CROP.

| CROP |
| ____ |
| ____ |
| ____ |
| ____ |
| SEED |

7 Baseball problem: What is the fewest number of pitches that a pitcher may throw and pitch a complete nine-inning game?

8 Music puzzle: Nine chords have been taken apart and the pitch names listed in the three columns below. Using each pitch once define the chords listed on the right.

Ab	C	F	Major Triad _____
Ab	C	F	Minor Triad _____
A	C	F	Augmented Triad _____
A	C	F	Diminished Triad _____
Bb	D	F	Dominant Seventh _____
Bb	D	F#	Dominant Ninth _____
B	D	G	Diminished Seventh _____
B	D	G	Supertonic Seventh _____
B	D	G	Augmented Sixth _____
B	D	G	
	D		
	D#		
	E		

9 Name the colors that would remain on a color wheel of twelve colors if you were to eliminate the primary and secondary colors.

Answers to the Brain Teases are available in the <u>Mass</u> <u>Media</u> Guide.

Were there some problems you skipped over because you knew you couldn't deal with them? What knowledge or skill were you lacking that caused you to skip them?

Did you start some problems, then quit working at them? Which ones? Why did you stop?

What was the maximum amount of time you spent with any one problem?

What factors caused you to stay with a problem?

___ The problem was easy, I thought I could solve it.

___ The problem was hard, it was a challenge to me.

___ The problem interested me because I knew something about the subject.

Would you have been better motivated and given more time and effort to the problems if you were graded on them?

If the problems were part of a quiz show in class?

If you were paid five dollars for each correct solution?

In view of the data which has emerged in this lab, how do you think the fact of thresholds affects the decisions of mass media editors and program directors?

Do you think these editors and program directors might feel any obligation to make audiences reach beyond their present thresholds?

LAB MY THRESHOLDS

Consider your own personal use of the mass media, the choice you make from day to day. See if you can indicate what factors in your life history have influenced your interests and readiness to make these choices. In other words, what are your present interest thresholds, and what determined them?

Some of my Thresholds

Media choices:	Influencing factors:
I like to read newspapers, books, and magazines.	I was able to read at four years old. We have many books at home.
I read the sports section in the paper and watch sports specials on TV.	My father loved sports and took me to games when I was young.

INTERFACE

The school's response to the fact of thresholds is usually tracking. What kinds of classroom materials are used in different tracks to accommodate different thresholds?

Whose thresholds are considered when magazines are ordered for the school library?

If certain classes in your school use TV broadcasts and periodicals in place of or along with textbooks, which broadcasts and periodicals are used? Are the choices popular with the students? Why or why not?

Do you think the disc jockey most listened to by teen-agers in your area underestimates his audience's interest in world events?

INVESTIGATE

1   Collect copies of a neighborhood newspaper, an ethnic newspaper, or a small-town weekly. COMPARE their challenge to reading skills and current events knowledge to the challenge posed by the Christian Science Monitor.

2   ANALYZE radio or TV talk shows. Do the hosts guide the conversations so as to keep up a steady demand on the audience, or does this fluctuate?

3   EVALUATE the need for a public broadcast network, one that does not depend on advertising revenues and mass audience support. Do the present public broadcast producers see themselves as serving people with "higher thresholds" than those who watch regular network shows?

Every year millions of young men and women leave home for the first time and find themselves in institutional food lines in colleges, boot camps, and corporations. Result: letters home for food parcels, angry letters to campus papers, and endless local jokes. Suddenly they find out how unique and individual their own tastes are.

The mass media by their very nature cannot cater to an individual's unique tastes. But then how does the individual respond? He picks and chooses from a wide variety of offerings. Have you ever considered how you pick and choose? How your tastes differ from mass popular tastes? Here's a chance to find out.

LAB CUSTOM-MADE MAGAZINE

Design a magazine to be published just for yourself. Put into the magazine all the articles, pictures, ads, stories, and cartoons that you would like to read. Don't include anything you would pass up in another magazine.

Here are some elements to consider and guidelines to follow as you design your magazine.

Title: It is your magazine; give it a unique title that suits you.

Frequency: How often will your magazine be published? Will it appear on a consistent date?

Format: Determine the size, shape, approximate number of pages, general use of photos, proportion of editorial to advertising material. Will you use a glossy or dull-finish paper? What typeface will you use for editorial content? What kind of type for headlines?

Editorial Profile: Write a paragraph describing the general interests of the audience (yourself) which could be printed in Writer's Guide as an indication to writers of the kind of manuscripts you are interested in receiving.

Advertising: What type of advertising will you accept, what products and services would you be happy to have your readers (you) informed about? Are there any ads you will refuse to accept? Prepare a paragraph suitable for Consumer Market, a publication used by ad agencies to find out what kind of advertising a magazine is interested in receiving.

Contents: List the articles, stories, and features that will appear in your first issue with a sentence or two describing each.

Cover: Use a separate paper or art board to design your cover. Execute the cover for the first issue. It should express the style and content of your magazine.

| PROSPECTUS OUTLINE OF MY MAGAZINE |

Title: Frequency:

Format:

Editorial Profile:

Advertising:

Contents:

The prospectus and cover you have created
should reflect your own individual tastes
in magazines. Is there a magazine on the
market now that offers most of the content
and style of your custom-made magazine?

If so, do you subscribe to it or buy it regularly?

If not, how do you satisfy your interests in these areas?

Share your prospectus and cover with five
or six others in the class.

Would others buy your magazine for eight
to ten dollars a year?

Would others in the group have developed
the same type of magazine for you as you
developed for yourself?

How is your magazine unique, original,
and specifically tailored to your needs?

Between 1959 and 1969, the number of American magazines offering specialized editions jumped from 126 to 235. Thus every large circulation magazine in the United States today prints slightly different editions for different regions of the country. . . . Furthermore, the rate of new magazine births has shot way up. . . . We are getting a richer mix, a far greater choice of magazines than ever before. ALVIN TOFFLER

The advance of communications technology is quietly and rapidly de-monopolizing communications without a shot being fired. The result is a rich destandardization of cultural output. . . . And technology, far from restricting our individuality, will multiply our choices—and our freedom —exponentially. ALVIN TOFFLER

As this mediocrity, which in the short term is economically profitable, fills the air, it creates appetites; it styles the nation's tastes just as advertising influences what we eat, smoke and drive. The stock answer of network apologists for the current television schedule is: "We give the people what they want," but what has actually happened is that those viewers who have been brainwashed select their own brand of popcorn, while those of more discerning taste give up watching or listening. FRED FRIENDLY

INTERFACE

Courses in schools are generally designed for fairly large numbers of students. Textbooks are published for those courses that
generally appear in all schools and attract many students. Do
you think these facts sometimes prevent courses from being offered which you individually would like to take? Name a few such
courses? What texts would you use?

Compare your local media with regional and national media. Are
the local media more responsive to your particular needs than the
regional or national media? How could you make the local media
more responsive to your needs?

INVESTIGATE

1   Check your local library for a list of books acquired in the past several months.
INTERVIEW the librarian to find out how these books are selected and how they discover the needs and tastes of the community.

2   INTERVIEW local theater managers to find out what policies govern the selection
of films shown in their theaters.

3   STUDY the audience survey methods of the television rating services, Nielsen
and ARB. Both companies have films and literature explaining their services.

You have explored some of the qualities of popular taste and investigated how audience thresholds affect media content. Publishers and broadcasters have at times been accused of simply giving the people what they want. Whether they can or should do something beyond this is a special question that will be taken up later. But there is a very legitimate sense in which publishers and broadcasters must respond to popular needs and desires or they will not survive. How do they find out what the people want? How do they measure popular taste and preferences? There are several ways of doing this. The following lab proposes one way, a Q-Sort survey.

LAB THE Q-SORT

There are plans to install a juke box in your school cafeteria, and you have been appointed to select records for it. You want to offer a variety of records that will appeal to the tastes of as many segments of the student body as you can. To find out and measure the different music tastes in the student population, you will run a Q-Sort survey.

Assign a number to every person who will participate in the survey and have him write his name on the grid that follows. If there are more than twenty-four, form two groups for the survey.

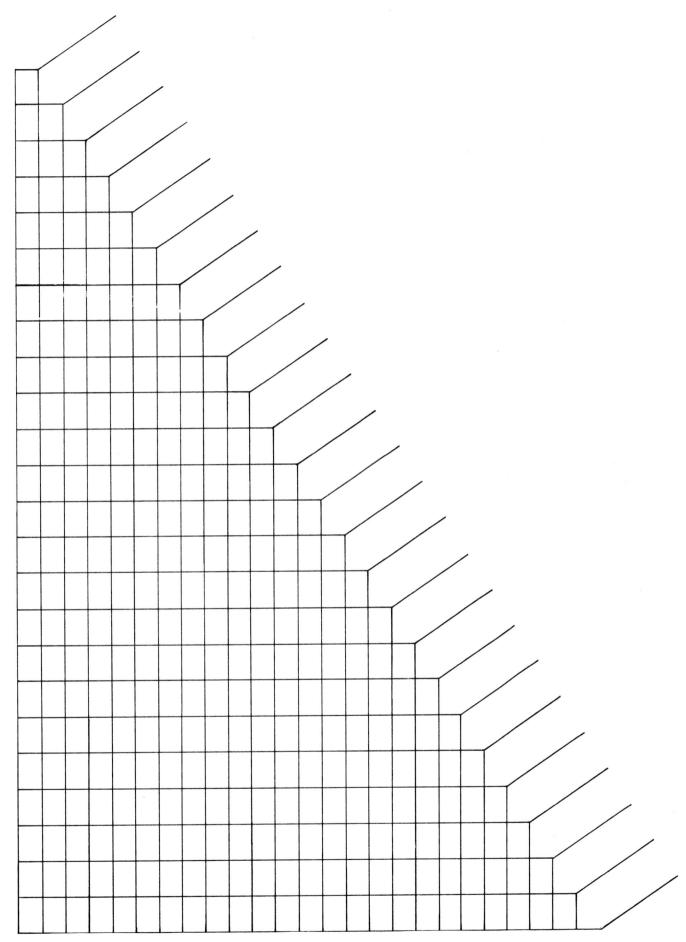

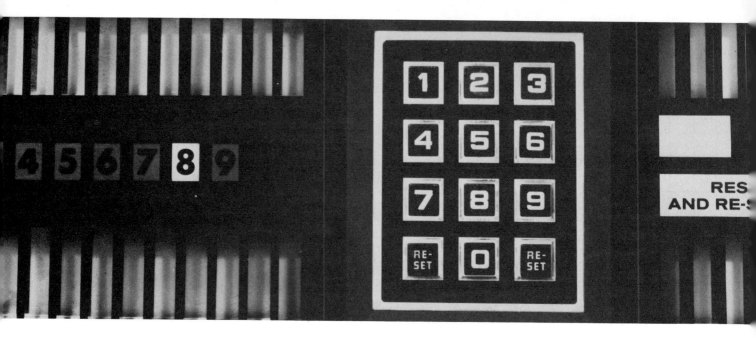

Next, make a list of 70 current record titles as possibilities for the juke box. For sorting purposes, put each title on a separate card or slip of paper. Each participant will have a stack of 70 cards which he is to sort into three different piles. One pile contains the ten record titles he would most like to listen to. A second pile contains the ten titles he least likes. The third pile contains the remaining cards.

Each person should then choose three from the top ten titles, his very best liked records, and three from the least liked, according to his tastes, the very worst. Then fill in the record titles as indicated on the chart below.

Best liked	Least liked
1	1
2	2
3	3
4	4
5	5
6	6
7	7
8	8
9	9
10	10

Since the purpose of the survey is to identify groups of people with similar tastes (so you can provide records for each taste group), each person in the survey will have to compare and correlate his choices with every other person in the survey.

Here is how two people would find their correlation score. For duplicate choices in the "very best" or "very worst" categories, score 2. For any other duplicate choices either in the "Best liked" or "Least liked" category, score 1. For example:

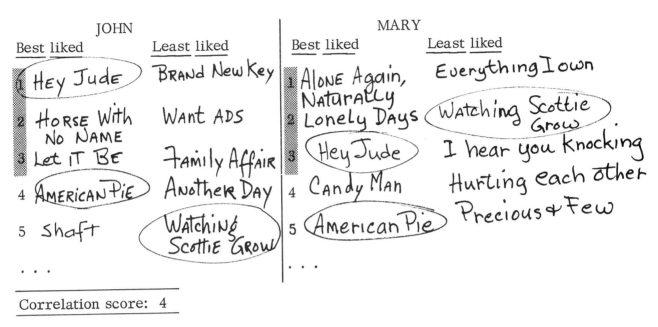

Correlation score: 4

Then John and Mary fill in this score on the large grid at the intersection where their names meet.

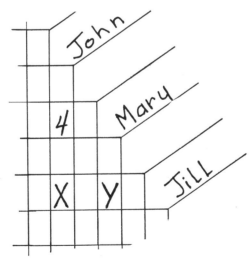

X is where the correlation score between John and Jill will go; Y is where the score between Mary and Jill will go. Fill in the grid with the correlation scores of all the students in the survey.

When all the correlation scores have been figured and recorded on the grid, each participant should examine the grid, find out which people he correlates highly with, and meet together with them.

What music tastes characterize the people in each cluster group? (For example, your group may like acid rock and dislike folk music.) Have each cluster group make up a descriptive label for itself. (E.g., Acid Rock Lovers) If two or more groups come up with similar labels, they should form into larger cluster groups.

List the cluster groups that form. These will be the dominant taste groups in your class.

Taste groups: Records for each group:

How many different record audiences did you find in your survey?

Were you surprised by the people who were gathered together with similar music tastes?

Could the clusters which emerged be used to predict other taste factors?

How could you use the information you have gathered in the survey to choose records for the juke box that would satisfy the tastes of most of the students?

If your choices do not correlate highly with anyone else's, what does this indicate about the taste patterns you have developed?

Why do you think NBC used a Q-Sort to discover the three main clusters of TV audiences?

INTERFACE

Do you think you could predict a friend's ten favorite TV shows?
Your father's? Your mother's? Try it.

If you were on a school dance committee, how would you go about
choosing the band that would appeal to most of the students?

Considering the different interest thresholds in the student body,
what activities should be included in the yearbook? Could you
measure the different interest groups?

INVESTIGATE

1   TALK to a local bookseller and ask him if sales (the popular taste) in your
community correspond to national best selling patterns.

2   INTERVIEW a radio broadcaster about his program practices. How does he
measure or find out what the people want to hear? How can he tell if his programming corresponds to his audience's tastes?

3   INTERVIEW one or other magazine seller in your neighborhood and ask him if
local sales (popular taste) in your community corresponds to the top circulation
patterns in the country.

4   FIND persons in your community who have taken part in audience measuring
or rating surveys. Ask them about their attitudes toward the measuring system.

5   INTERVIEW a local theater manager. How does he measure popular taste in
movies in your community? What do his box office figures reveal?

It would be naive to think there is a direct relation between popular taste and mass media editing and programming. There is another factor in this equation, the economic support of the advertiser. Magazines derive approximately 59 percent of their revenues from advertising, newspapers 74 percent, and radio and television 100 percent.

Readers, listeners, and viewers are consumers with buying power, even if they only read the funnies or listen to hard rock. Advertisers want to reach as many of these potential buyers as possible. Your favorite magazine, radio station, or TV program competes to attract as many people as possible so they can interest more advertisers at higher rates to buy their space or time. There is a circle of interlocking relationships: editing and programming, popular taste, advertising support.

There may have been a time when the advertiser was simply interested in getting his message to the greatest number of people. Today the wise media buyer wants to target his advertising message to a specific group of people within the total media audience. He chooses the medium and the time that will most efficiently get his message to his potential buyer.

The labs which follow are designed to help you identify some of the special interest segments within the vast media audience.

 RADIO QUIZ

Who listens to the radio? Have a team of students tape record ahead of time one or two _characteristic_ minutes of sound from ten different radio stations. Have them play the tape for the class. This is a radio quiz: Fill in the blanks below with the call letters of as many stations as you can recognize from their sounds alone.

1 _____   6 _____

2 _____   7 _____

3 _____   8 _____

4 _____   9 _____

5 _____   10 _____

 **AM-FM AUDIENCES**

How many different audiences does radio serve? Listen on the AM, then on the FM dial, moving from one end of the frequency band to the other. List the stations you hear, the format they use, type of music played, special features, and advertisements. Listen to each station for ten minutes at least to get the necessary information and fill in the chart below. Finally estimate the type of audience each station reaches. (If there are a large number of stations in your area, divide them up among the students, two or three to each.)

Call letters	Format	Music	Special features	Advertisers	Audience
WZYX	music, news, comment	middle of the road, easy listening	stock market reports	airlines, real estate, local shops	suburban housewives, men in business

How does one station's audience change through the day? through the week? Who listens on Sunday at 10 a.m.? Saturday at 3 p.m.? Any afternoon at 3 p.m.? Any evening at midnight?

How do AM and FM stations differ in program policies in general?

Does the time allotted to advertising differ on AM and FM stations? Are the rates different? Why?

What are the technical differences between AM and FM broadcasting? How do they differ in power and range?

The editorial profiles printed below indicate how a few popular magazines understand themselves and their readership. These profiles come from the Standard Rate and Data Service's (SRDS) book Consumer Magazine and Farm Publication Rates and Data.

Ebony

PUBLISHER'S EDITORIAL PROFILE

EBONY is a black-oriented, general, picture magazine dealing primarily with contemporary topics. Feature articles deal with education, history, politics, literature, art, business, personalities, civil rights, sports, entertainment, music and social events. Regular monthly departments include "Speaking of People," "Fashion Fair," "Photo-Editorial," "Sounds" (record review), "Ebony Book Shelf," and "Date With a Dish" (culinary art). The August issue is devoted to an in-depth treatment of one aspect of current life in Black America such as civil rights, youth, segregation.

Life

PUBLISHER'S EDITORIAL PROFILE

LIFE is a people to people magazine, about things that affect people today. The editorial goal is to sort out, put in perspective and add personal significance to stories and events whose importance is best defined by the use of pictures and words. LIFE attempts to make the reader aware of the important occurances in an environment of ceaseless change and extravagant communication.

Seventeen

PUBLISHER'S EDITORIAL PROFILE

SEVENTEEN Magazine is edited for the nation's teen-age girls. Feature articles run the gamut from reports on high school literary magazines and teen drinking to a discussion of getting along with parents. Regular monthly departments include fashion, beauty, entertainment, home, food, etiquette, "You the Reader" teen news and contributions, and a celebrity 'talk to teens'' series. Monthly columns include reviews of new movies, TV shows, recordings and books; travel; college and careers. Almost every month SEVENTEEN publishes three short stories.

Esquire

PUBLISHER'S EDITORIAL PROFILE

ESQUIRE is edited for a wide range of masculine interests. Monthly features include articles on travel and fashion, literary fiction, and reviews of books, records and films. The major portion of the editorial content of each issue is devoted to articles and special features on sports, personalities, satire, recreation, the performing arts, alcoholic beverages, automotive topics, current social and political affairs, and a variety of other contemporary subjects.

Newsweek

PUBLISHER'S EDITORIAL PROFILE

NEWSWEEK surveys the world's news for people with an abiding interest in the week's events, departmented into 20 sections, from National Affairs to Movies, Music, Books, and Art. Periscope includes behind-the-scene highlights, plus forecasts of things to come. Wall Street and Spotlight On Business, are of particular interest to business readers. Also featured are distinguished columnists writing on national and international developments, on the Washington scene, on the economy.

Ski

PUBLISHER'S EDITORIAL PROFILE

SKI magazine is edited for U. S. and Canadian skiers, with attention given to editorial fare for both the new skier as well as the expert. Instruction and technique articles are prepared by North American and European ski instructors. Travel articles feature color photography, plus columns of travel tips. Personality profiles cover racers, coaches and skiers. Adventure stories in the high mountains. Consumer advice articles on what's new in equipment. Humorous articles and cartoons. Regional reports from international staff of correspondents, plus ski film and book reviews, fashion, shopper items, question-and-answer columns for readers on instruction, equipment repair

Grit

PUBLISHER'S EDITORIAL PROFILE

GRIT is edited for small town families. It is a picture magazine (over 100 illustrations each week). It is a news magazine with a news review tailored to fit the thinking of small town families. GRIT is a woman's magazine with features on food, style, beauty, household helps, child care and other items which interest women. With fiction, a weekly sermon, sports, comics and other features, GRIT is devoted to the interests of the small town family. GRIT regularly reviews and presents stories on progressive developments in small towns throughout the country.

Popular Science

PUBLISHER'S EDITORIAL PROFILE

POPULAR SCIENCE concentrates its editorial on new products that may be of special usefulness and importance to its readers—men with strong interests in their homes, their personal transportation needs, and in recreation. Each month, the magazine reports on products still on industrial drawing boards. It also introduces readers to products already in the marketplace. And it provides "use" suggestions about products that readers may already own. Major articles and departmental features cover such product areas as automobiles; boats and engines; home workshop tools; garden and lawn equipment; electronic, TV, and photographic equipment; and recreation products.

Sports Illustrated

PUBLISHER'S EDITORIAL PROFILE

SPORTS ILLUSTRATED reports and interprets each week the world of sport, recreation and active leisure. It previews, analyzes and comments upon major games and events, as well as those noteworthy for character and spirit alone. It features individuals important to sport and evaluates trends important to the part sport plays in contemporary life. It provides instruction for both participants and spectators. Articles range through many fields essential to a comprehensive exposition of sport: travel, architecture, art, fashion, physical fitness and conservation. Special departments deal with shops, sports equipment, books and statistics. SPORTS ILLUSTRATED uses color photography and specially commissioned art profusely

LADIES' HOME JOURNAL

PUBLISHER'S EDITORIAL PROFILE

LADIES' HOME JOURNAL is a personal magazine for women, edited to supply information and inspiration to the younger woman on her worlds of fashion, homemaking, personal appearance, and current interests. The subject matter ranges, literally, from pickles to politics — to provide a balance of interests in women's lives. The distinctive aspect of the JOURNAL's approach is its extensive use of the case-history technique, as witness such monthly departments as "How America Lives" and "Can This Marriage Be Saved?" The subjects of food, fashion, and homemaking account for better than half of each month's editorial fare.

Reader's Digest

PUBLISHER'S EDITORIAL PROFILE

READER'S DIGEST is a general interest, non-fiction reading magazine for the entire family. Half of the articles are "digested" from articles appearing in other publications. The balance is staff-written or contributed by readers and each issue carries a condensation of a current book. Article subjects include: self improvement, psychology, ecology, government, world affairs, crime, community action, health. "Unforgettable Characters," campus, employment, sports, travel, science and invention, "Word Power," "Humor in Uniform" and other broad-interest subjects.

'Teen

PUBLISHER'S EDITORIAL PROFILE

'TEEN is edited for young, active, first impression teenage girls. Features and departments deal with improving beauty and grooming care, current fashions, exercise and diet guidance, boy/girl relations, dating, careers and other subjects that will aid in the development of the reader. Fashion and beauty guidance is approximately one-half editorial content, with balance in features, entertainment and fiction. Special features include: Dear Beauty Editor, Enter-'TEENment Mailbag, Teens in the News, Sex and Dating, Dear Jack, Dear Jill, MD's Corner, Rapping on Records, 'Teen Tested Topics and My Fair and Frantic Hollywood, Your Horoscope and We Get. Two fiction stores are published monthly.

Each consumer magazine addresses itself to a certain segment of the general reading public. Get a copy of one of these magazines and bring it to class. See if the issue you bring meets the publisher's description as you have read it.

Which articles or features specifically accomplish the stated purpose? Is there anything in the magazine which conflicts with the expressed editorial policy?

How does the advertising conform to the editorial policy and the intended readership?

How many magazines do you know of that are published specifically for teen-age readers and subscribers? Do you read any of them? What advantages do they have for you? What kinds of advertising do they carry?

PROFESSIONAL AND TRADE JOURNALS

In the previous lab you dealt with a variety of consumer magazines published for the general reading public. But most of the magazine industry in the United States publishes professional journals, trade magazines, and specialty magazines for highly defined, special interest audiences. American Medical Association Bulletin, Harvard Law Review, American Psychologist, Journal of the American Bar Association, Publications of the Modern Language Association are all professional journals. Billboard, Television/Radio Age, Women's Wear Daily, Broadcasting, Architectural Record, Advertising Age, Amusement Business, Chemical Week, Publishers' Weekly, Purchasing, Vend are all trade magazines.

Ask someone in your family or a neighbor to get you a back issue of one or other professional or trade publications from his office or plant. Evaluate each magazine according to the chart below. Bring all these publications to school and display them in your classroom or library. Select a variety of magazines and pool the data from several of them on the chart below.

Title	Frequency	Audience	Contents	Type of advertising
Vend	monthly	food service operators, vending companies, amusement contractors	news, development in the field, "How To" features	65% advertising, vending machines, machine makers, concession companies, food suppliers

**FOCUS**

Does your school library receive any
professional journals or trade magazines?
Which ones?

Do you or does any member of your family receive any of these magazines. Which
ones?

What do you notice about the vocabulary
in a professional or trade journal? Cite
instances of specialized or technical
vocabulary.

Read through an article in one of the
journals brought to class. How does
your knowledge of the vocabulary relate
to your interest threshold in that field?

What did you notice about the advertising
in the professional or trade journals you
examined? How did the ads differ from
those in consumer magazines? Any ads for
the same product, different ads for different audiences?

 **NEWSPAPERS**

Bring to class copies of any newspaper you know of which is published for a specific
ethnic, occupational, religious, or foreign language readership. List them below.

Paper	Special Readership	Advertising
Wall Street Journal	*Businessmen*	*Banks, Corporations, Stock offers*

Examine copies of the papers cited above. Pass them around the class. Note whether the advertising in the papers reflects the special interests of the readership.

 **TV DEMOGRAPHICS**

Who watches what on television? Research companies such as the A. C. Nielsen Company and the American Research Bureau publish demographic tables which tell advertisers which specific audience groups watch which TV programs throughout the day and week. With this information advertisers can target their commercial messages to their most likely potential customers.

Some standard audience categories are listed below. Under each audience segment write down what you think are the five most popular prime time TV programs for that group.

Children 2-11

_____

_____

_____

_____

_____

Men 18-49

_____

_____

_____

_____

_____

Adults 50 -

_____

_____

_____

_____

_____

Teens 12-17

_____

_____

_____

_____

_____

Women 18-49

_____

_____

_____

_____

_____

Now make your own survey of some people you know in each category to find out what their favorite TV programs are. Tabulate an average and list these programs below. Compare your estimates with your survey results. Compare your survey results with others in the class.

Children 2-11

_____

_____

_____

_____

_____

Men 18-49

_____

_____

_____

_____

_____

Adults 50 -

_____

_____

_____

_____

_____

Teens 12-17

_____

_____

_____

_____

_____

Women 18-49

_____

_____

_____

_____

_____

Now check your estimate and your survey results against the latest national rating figures of the A. C. Nielsen Company supplied with the Mass Media Guide.

Children 2-11

_____
_____
_____
_____

Teens 12-17

_____
_____
_____
_____

Men 18-49

_____
_____
_____
_____

Women 18-49

_____
_____
_____
_____

Adults 50 -

_____
_____
_____
_____

Using the latest Nielsen ratings of the most popular programs in each audience category, make task forces to watch these programs and note the commercials on them. How do the commercials relate to the audience groups?

Ages:	Program:		Commercials:
Children 2-11	1	_____	_____
	2	_____	_____
	3	_____	_____
	4	_____	_____
	5	_____	_____
Teens 12-17	1	_____	_____
	2	_____	_____
	3	_____	_____
	4	_____	_____
	5	_____	_____
Men 18-49	1	_____	_____
	2	_____	_____
	3	_____	_____
	4	_____	_____
	5	_____	_____
Women 18-49	1	_____	_____
	2	_____	_____
	3	_____	_____
	4	_____	_____
	5	_____	_____
Adults 50 -	1	_____	_____
	2	_____	_____
	3	_____	_____
	4	_____	_____
	5	_____	_____

INTERFACE

What media does your school use to advertise games, dances, plays, and other activities? Do these media reach the audiences you need to reach? What better use of the media could you propose?

The largest segment of the American population is the post World War II baby boom. During the 1960's advertisers courted this large youth audience with all possible appeal and interest. Now that this group is getting older, do you see any evidence that certain advertising is changing from youth appeal to more established advertising patterns in order to keep up with the changing interests of this large audience group?

INVESTIGATE

1   Call or visit your nearest radio station. Ask for a public relations man or the station manager. INQUIRE how they find out who is listening to their station and how they use this information to plan programming and solicit advertising.

2   Many FM stations are owned by companies which also own AM stations. DO the owners seek different special audiences with their different stations?

3   We all complain about the amount of advertising that interrupts the Top 40 or the Thursday night TV movie. But we usually do not know for sure just how much advertising there is in each media in proportion to the editorial and creative content. FORM investigative teams to make in-depth analyses of the advertising-to-editorial ratios in each of the major media examined above. You may be surprised by your findings.

Radio: Call or visit a local radio station and INQUIRE how many minutes per hour of programming is allotted to commercials. Calculate the percentage of advertising to regular programming and note the figure in the chart below.

Newspaper: TAKE your daily newspaper for a week. Note the total number of pages in each issue. Then go through and figure out how much space is given to advertising in each issue. Add up your figures and work out the percentage of advertising to editorial content in each issue of the paper. Note that the word editorial in this context refers to anything in the paper which is not advertising.

Newspaper:

Day:	Total pages:	Pages of advertising:	Percentage:
Monday			
Tuesday			
Wednesday			
Thursday			
Friday			
Saturday			
Sunday			

Magazine: Select a consumer magazine and CALCULATE the percentage of advertising to editorial content as with the newspapers above. Place the percentages on the master chart below.

Television: The time allotted for advertising messages on commercial television is controlled by the Television Code of the National Association of Broadcasters. The regulations read as follows: "In prime time, non-program material shall not exceed 10 minutes in any 60-minute period. . . . In all other time, non-program material shall not exceed 16 minutes in any 60-minute period." CALCULATE the percentage of commercials to program time on TV as you did for the other media and enter the percentage figures for a prime time hour in the master chart below.

Percentage of Advertising

Radio:	Newspaper:	Magazine:	Television:

Where I Stand -

Based on your experience with the units in this section, which of the following positions seems better to you?

a) I believe that schools should concentrate on educating people's tastes. If schools accomplish this, we will have mass media that elevate and challenge taste rather than the mass pulp we have today.	b) I believe that the mass media really reflect the wide diversity of taste in our society. I don't think any public system, schools or government, should prescribe what is good taste. I want to be able to respect my own tastes and those of others. If I should influence others' tastes or be influenced by theirs, that's just part of the interaction.

SIMULATE

Using the insights and conclusions you arrived at above, role play the following Media Man Simulation.

You are the manager of a movie theater, one of forty in a four-state area owned and operated by Film World, Inc. Film World makes the bookings for all the theaters in its central office. The only thing you do with regard to booking is to request that a film be held over in your theater if it has been especially successful at the box office. Otherwise, you manage the building, arrange publicity, manage the concessions, hire personnel, and deal with complaints.

Two months ago you exhibited an "X" rated movie that did remarkably well at the box office, but a controversy ensued because the PTA charged the movie contained "excessive violence and nudity." You received ten angry phone calls and several church organizations planned public censures and boycotts.

Now another film is due to be shown in your theater that has many of the same characteristics as the one which caused the controversy. You have previewed the film, advance publicity is on display in your lobby, and now representatives of the PTA and several church groups want to see you this afternoon. How will you deal with them?

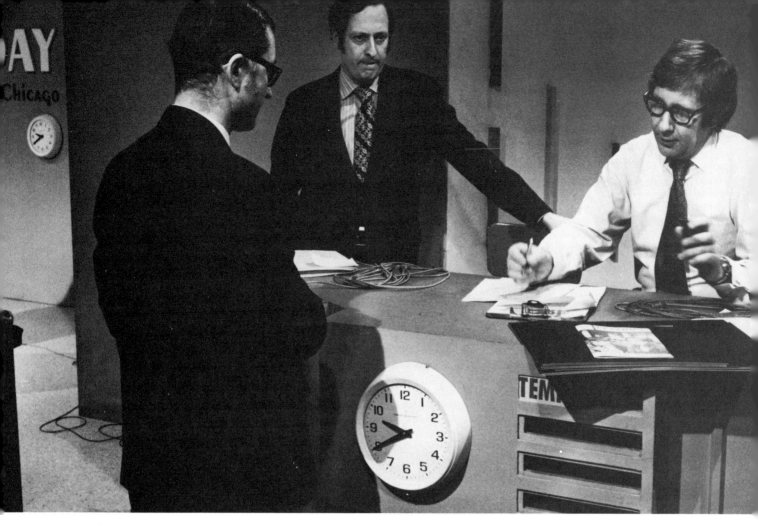

The Decision Makers

Half a program director's job is coming up with new shows. The other half, some would say the other 90%, is in knowing how to design a weekly schedule, in knowing where to put shows to attract maximum audiences.

THOMAS THOMPSON

Much advertising is purchased scientifically. The advertiser knows his product appeals to a certain kind of people. He wants to reach as many of them as possible for a given amount of money. A study of circulations, ratings, and audience surveys tells him which media reach the highest percentage of his customers most efficiently. To make certain of broad coverage he may use more than one medium.

RICHARD FRISBIE

The only available measure of success is audience size. And the only way of measuring that is the rating system, upon which the entire financial structure of television rests.

RICHARD TOWNLEY

PROBE

How do media men understand their audiences?

At this point you have probed the tastes of the mass audiences as they come to the media smorgasbord. You've found them with their peanut butter and jelly and with their caviar. Now it's time to meet the caterers, the media men and women who make up the menus and display their wares before the public consumers.

These men and women are the editors and program directors, the producers and publishers, the directors and owners, the gatekeepers who make the decisions on what media fare will be served.

What we wish to find out in this lab is what these people think about us, the mass audiences. Who do they think we are? How do they find out what we want to see and hear and read? How do they perceive our tastes? What are the factors that enter into their decision making?

The lab takes the form of a Jackdaw, a collection of primary source material, personal remarks, direct quotations, writings of the people themselves who make these decisions. No writer stands between you and the original, as often happens in social science textbooks. Using the material as bits of truth, you can put them together like a jigsaw puzzle in order to get some vision of the whole picture. But don't stop there, the more original data you can bring to the lab, the better your picture will be and the more reliable your conclusions.

 ## THE MEDIA MAN'S JACKDAW

The Jackdaw consists of first-person statements by decision makers from four different media: magazines, movies, television, and newspapers. After each input you'll find a couple of questions to focus the inquiry, and at the end a cumulative data sheet for recording your general conclusions.

It will be most helpful for you to expand the inquiry beyond the given material by writing or interviewing media decision makers in your own area. Ask them how they find out the needs and tastes of their audiences, and how they make their decisions.

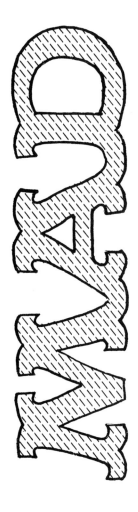

Why is MAD so popular with youth?

I think it's because they believe that we understand their problems and that we call a spade a spade. We seem to be able to remain free of pressure and, therefore, they probably feel that we are honest enough to appraise a situation in its true sense.

How do you keep MAD young in spirit?

Gee, I don't know. The whole group of us here is getting older. But I think all this "generation gap" thing is a lot of baloney. Age is not the determining factor. What's wrong is lack of communication. After all, old people can communicate, too. Let's face it, some of the leaders of the younger generation are over 30. And have been for a long time.

The answer to communicating with youth is the answer to the question: "Is what you're saying honest?" Are you touching the youth? Are you listening to them? Are you feeling their problems, their fears, their anxieties? Motivation of some kind is what makes people behave. No matter how old I get, I'm always going to be conscious of the fact that today's kids are growing up with fears and anxieties that older people cannot really understand because it wasn't the same in their younger days.

When I was young, my fear was economic. "How will I go about making a living when I grow up?" War for me was one bullet that might hit me if I was involved in it. Today the kids ask, "Will I ever grow up?" for they are involved with possible total annihilation in the hands of someone they have no control over. The odds against the youth are frightening.

Has youth's sense of humor changed over the years?

Absolutely. They're more serious, if you can say there is such a thing as a serious sense of humor. In terms of youthful humor, it's more of a reaction than a belly laugh. For example, in a recent issue of MAD we saluted the output of U.S. industry by showing a factory belching out balls of smoke that formed into skulls personifying death. Now that's not intrinsically funny, yet there's an appreciation of it because we're saying things that the young person feels. It's a truth. They get a kind of kick out of it which isn't necessarily a belly-laugh kick.

Do you feel the culture is maturing?

It's growing, but I'm not sure whether it's maturing. I mean that sex for sex's sake is not necessarily mature. I think these young movie producers are trying to brutalize sex in order to brutalize old people. They're saying, "Well, look how shocking we can get, you old fogies. See what your standards are these days." It's symbolic, but that doesn't necessarily mean it's right. But it's like a pendulum swinging back and forth and when we find a middle area, we'll be OK.

Albert B. Feldstein
Editor, MAD Magazine

Both editors point out that they are honest with their readers. Do they mean the same thing by the word "honest"?

What methods do the editors use to keep in touch with their audiences?

Do you feel that these editors have a good idea of who you are, where you are, and what you want?

How would you describe a typical SEVENTEEN reader?

We feel that there really is no such thing as a "typical" SEVENTEEN reader. All people are individuals. However, there are certain key denominators that apply to the majority of the 6.9 million girls between 13 and 19 who read SEVENTEEN each month.

They are idealistic. They veto glamour jobs in favor of "do unto others" posts (for example, an estimated 22.4% want to teach and another 19.2% envision themselves as future Dr. Kildares and Florence Nightingales). They know what they want, whether merchandise or the kind of man they want to marry. An overwhelming majority, 10.5 million, desire a college education. And they all want to look their best and act their best.

Why is SEVENTEEN popular with youth?

We feel our popularity is due to the fact that we are always honest with our readers. We cover their interests—beauty, fashion, boys, news of what their peers are doing. We never talk down to them. We try to guide them in their learning process without being painful or boring about it. WE NEVER TALK DOWN TO THEM. We tell them what their mother's can't, or won't, tell them. They view us as a helpful older sister.

How do you keep SEVENTEEN young in spirit?

We listen to what youth has to say and then act upon it. Our editors travel constantly, speaking to young people the length and breadth of the United States. We have 692 teen boards whom we question constantly to learn what is new in their communities. We do constant research on a variety of subjects to learn what people want. For instance, recently we did a survey of 2000 boys and girls, ages 14-22, to learn what they think is "Right and Wrong with America."

Have youth's tastes changed much over the years?

Youth itself has changed and SEVENTEEN has changed with youth. Today youth stands as the moral conscience of the nation. To paraphrase F. Scott Fitzgerald, today's young people are different from you and me and we had better learn from that difference. The fact that SEVENTEEN has changed shows that we have learned.

Some changes: Teen-agers have a different feeling about money than adults. Adults have been touched by depressions. Teens have not. They feel money is meant to be spent. Their life goals are different. What they want most is to help others not to reap profits as a corporation head. They demand revolution in education. Subjects and courses that are not pertinent in today's times simply bore students. They identify with the poor minority groups.

While other magazines decline and fall, SEVENTEEN is a success story. Why? Because as teens have changed, we have changed our content. As late as July 1965, we ran an article "Love and Sex" that answered such questions as "Does a contract for a date include a good night kiss clause?" and "What's the difference between necking and petting?" In October 1971 we ran an article titled "Is Virginity Outmoded?"

Ten years ago we answered questions like "Can a girl be too popular?" and "What Makes a Party Perk?" Today we write about volunteer programs like Sesame Street's Big Sisters who help inner city youngsters. Because so many teen girls marry young we are instituting a new supplement for "nearlyweds and newlyweds." We constantly add new columns. The latest "Nature's Table" which takes up what's new in natural foods.

Rosemary McMurtry
Editor, SEVENTEEN Magazine

I believe that everyone has to find truth for himself. It is completely useless to make a film with a message for everyone. I think it is immoral (in the true sense of the word) to tell a story that has a conclusion—you cut out your audience the moment you present a solution on the screen because there are no ready "solutions" in most of their lives. I think it is more moral—and more important— to show, let's say, the story of one man. Then everyone with his own sensibility and on the basis of his own inner development, can try to find his own solution. . . .

I seek to illuminate those things which I do not understand about myself, but since I am a man, other men (no doubt) can also discover themselves in this mirror as well. Any research that a man does about himself, about his relationships with others and with the mystery of life, is a spiritual and—in a true sense— religious search. In this search, I ask thought-provoking questions in a time when religious issues are once more becoming vital to ordinary people. If I can do no more than provide a "hint of an explanation" to the problems I raise, I have done quite a lot.

Frederico Fellini

Audiences are now quicker in perceiving the symbolic implications of a film than they were in the past, due to their watching television in general and TV commercials in particular. A film maker must always avoid consciously presenting an audience with a message that is preached at them. He should make a point, but one that is wrapped up in the dramatic situation.

John Schlesinger

SAMUEL GOLDWYN STUDIOS

Do the filmmakers specify their audiences as to age and interest as much as the magazine editors do?

Are these film directors more interested in responding to an audience or in having an audience respond to them? How does the film as a medium seem to affect this?

If you were a film director, what would you try to do, and what would be your attitude toward your audience?

There is so much talk about having something to say. Anyway, the people who have would probably want to write books, not direct films.

So much of the avant garde work these days is simply a diary, self-indulgent, lacking the basic development of plot and character.

I must say I like good dramatic construction. And I like to be excited when I go to the movies. I like to be touched. And I like a good yarn, I suppose.

David Lean

Capital Productions, Inc.

My point in all this kind of satire is that you really have to go out and woo the enemy. I can make a film where all the people who agree with me will come in and agree. That doesn't mean anything. But if I can get all the people who totally oppose me to expose themselves to certain material and laugh, and it's gotten into their computer, then later on they're just a little closer to the center of the argument. And you have to trick them into it.

I'm trying to reach toward a picture, I don't think I'll ever succeed but somebody will, a picture that's totally emotional—not narrative or intellectual—where the audience walks out and can't tell anything about it except what they feel—like the impact of a really great painting—like the first time I ever saw an original Monet. I didn't know who he was, I only knew I didn't want to leave it. I was almost oblivious to the content matter. I want to make a film where the effect not the story is what people carry with them when they leave the theater.

Robert Altman

I'm convinced that you can't change anyone's mind with a movie. However, I do believe that you can stimulate people to think about a problem—to perhaps consider it from another angle. It is my hope that people can come out of a theater thinking "Well, I never thought of it in just that way before." . . . I try to throw a searchlight on a problem; we can't pretend to solve it, but we *can* illuminate it from one angle.

Stanley Kramer

One of the reasons I'm still working is that people seem grateful that Lucy is there, the same character and unchanging view. There's so much chaos in this world, that's important. Many people, not only shut-ins, depend on the tube, too much so—they look for favorites they can count on. Older people loved Lawrence Welk. They associated his music with their youth. Now he's gone. It's not fair. They shouldn't have taken off those bucolic comedies; that left a big dent in some folks' lives. Maybe we're not getting messages anymore from the clergy, the politicians, so TV does the preaching. But as an entertainer, I don't believe in messages.

Years ago, the Romans let humans be eaten by lions, while they laughed and drank—that was entertainment. But I'm tired of the ugly. Fred Astaire and Ginger Rogers dancing, that's my idea of entertainment. Anything Richard Burton does is heaven. *Easy Rider* scared me at first because I knew how it could influence kids. But at least that movie came full circle. They led a life of nothing and they got nothing.

Lucille Ball

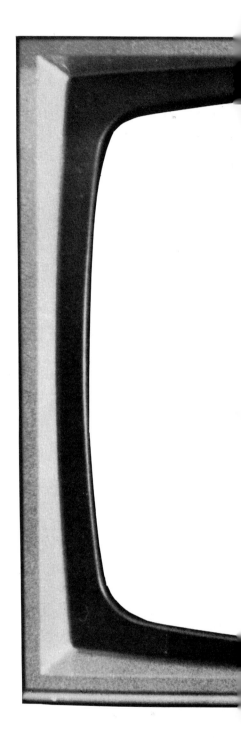

Unseen, and seldom sung, the television program director is the power behind the TV set in hundreds of communities. His are the decisions that change the copy in those millions of program guides week after week; he gets the blame, though seldom the praise. And oddly enough, the articles, studies, and books on the business focus on his job no more than the cameras do. J. DAVID LEWIS

TV network audiences are much larger than magazine or film audiences. How does this affect the program decision making?

What do you think Silverman means when he says he must answer to "public responsibility" and "to a country that's falling apart"?

Do you think a program director has any obligation to give the people something more than "just what they want"?

I bought "Z" because I think it should be seen. It says something that's important. I hope people will watch it, but it's a movie that should be seen.

BARRY DILLER, ABC-TV *movie director*

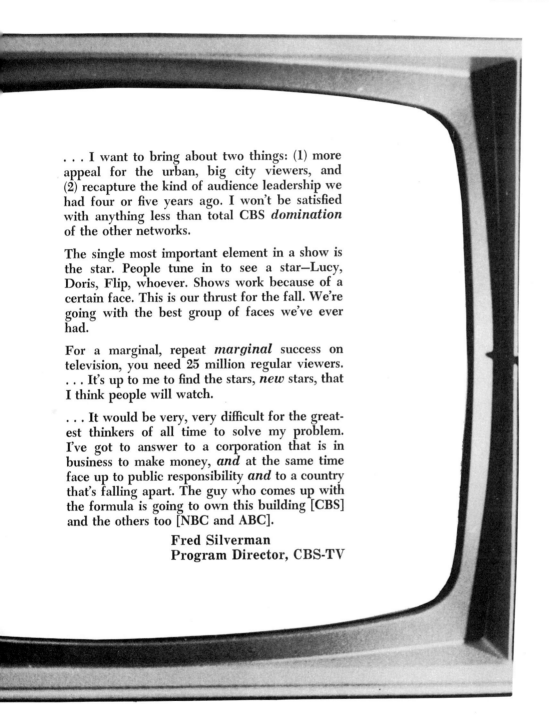

. . . I want to bring about two things: (1) more appeal for the urban, big city viewers, and (2) recapture the kind of audience leadership we had four or five years ago. I won't be satisfied with anything less than total CBS *domination* of the other networks.

The single most important element in a show is the star. People tune in to see a star—Lucy, Doris, Flip, whoever. Shows work because of a certain face. This is our thrust for the fall. We're going with the best group of faces we've ever had.

For a marginal, repeat *marginal* success on television, you need 25 million regular viewers. . . . It's up to me to find the stars, *new* stars, that I think people will watch.

. . . It would be very, very difficult for the greatest thinkers of all time to solve my problem. I've got to answer to a corporation that is in business to make money, *and* at the same time face up to public responsibility *and* to a country that's falling apart. The guy who comes up with the formula is going to own this building [CBS] and the others too [NBC and ABC].

Fred Silverman
Program Director, CBS-TV

Already he [Fred Silverman, CBS program director] is a wunderkind of his trade—conceiving and putting on the air television programs that he thinks people will watch. Note the sophisticated difference here: not programs that he thinks people will necessarily like, or benefit from, or be enriched by, but programs that he thinks people will watch.

THOMAS THOMPSON

Sports Highlights

TODAY

Florida's Space Age Newspaper

Published by The Garnett Company in Brevard County, Florida

Next Space

10 Cents

How would you describe your reading audience?

Aerospace workers form the backbone of our circulation, with a few military and retirees mixed in.

How do you decide what your audience needs to know?

I have periodic meetings with department heads and discuss coverage in general. We have a daily news meeting to determine which news shall be used. There is no other local morning daily in the Cape area; [If our paper ceased publication] our readers would be at a loss for local news, as they were before the paper was founded six years ago.

Do you feel an obligation to foster reader interest in newsworthy topics, or is this just their own responsibility?

We do not hesitate to promote, kind of, newsworthy topics which we feel are for the betterment of our community, such as cultural events, etc.

Do you sense any changes in your audience over the last five years, and if so, how have you responded to the changes?

Yes. Our audience's average age has "grown" 4-5 years. As a result, our newspaper is not produced solely for the young swingers (average age 26) that began the moon program. We do this with more retiree, business, and tourism news and have cut down on the amusements, sex, sin, crime, and other more sensational topics.

Robert Bentley
Editor, TODAY
Cape Kennedy, Florida

FOCUS

Do these newspaper men seem to have a better defined idea of who their audiences are than the magazine, film, and TV decision makers?

Do the newspaper decision makers seem more concerned about what their audiences like in a newspaper, or what they need in a newspaper?

Analyze and compare the statements of the two editors about their obligation to foster reader interest in newsworthy topics.

64

How would you describe your reading audience?

We feel we have a reasonably accurate view of the audience we are trying to reach with our papers. This was arrived at by both ordinary research and polling techniques and by more subjective evaluations by experienced journalists. The audience for our Sunday and daily Register has a more statewide and higher economic and educational character than the more localized audience of the afternoon Tribune. Because the Tribune circulates mostly in metropolitan Des Moines where the household coverage is over 80 per cent, we are talking about an audience that is virtually the same as the total population of the community. Because the bulk of The Register circulation is outside of the Des Moines area; and therefore in the areas where other more-local newspapers are distributed, we feel our audience tends to be somewhat different . . . they tend to be in a higher economic bracket and also tend to be interested in a level of news coverage which is beyond that offered by the local paper.

How do you decide what your audience needs to know?

Through a continuing system of research polling, we are asking our readers regularly about their needs and desires in terms of information coverage. Obviously, we feel our readers would suffer an information loss if the publications should cease. We look upon that loss to range from the absence of information about how their governments work (an essential in representative government) to the loss of information on stock market results, sporting information, advertising bargains, and home buying data.

Do you feel an obligation to foster reader interest in newsworthy topics, or is this just their own responsibility?

We feel we have an obligation to cover both events in which the readers have an interest naturally and those in which we may feel they should have information. By clear writing and innovative display, we feel we can attract enough attention to get their interest. We have an obligation to try to arouse interest, both from the idealistic viewpoint of the public's right to know and from the more practical side that if they aren't interested we won't stay in business very long.

Do you sense any changes in your audience over the last five years, and if so, how have you responded to the changes?

We feel there is a change of focus and possibly an increase in the range of interests that our audience has now over five years ago. We feel there is a turning inward on the part of some of our readers—an interest in more local problems over which the reader feels he can exercise some control and less interest in international problems which appear to the individual to be out of his control. We feel this turning inward manifests itself also in a broadening of subjects in which at least a portion of our audience have an interest. The explosion in the types of outdoor activities is an example.

A. Edward Heins
Managing Editor, THE REGISTER and TRIBUNE
Des Moines, Iowa

65

CUMULATIVE DATA SHEET

	Magazines	Movies	Television	Newspapers
How do the decision makers discover their audience's tastes?				
Do they try to respond to their audience's tastes?				
Do they try to influence their audience's tastes? If so, in what ways?				

INTERFACE

When you make a speech or a class presentation, or when you assist in producing a school program or publication (play, newspaper, yearbook, half-time show), what thought do you give to your audience? How do you find out "where they are"? How do you discover what their needs and tastes are? Did you ever try to give them something they "should" see or hear rather than something you know they want to see or hear?

What means are used in your school to discover what courses the students wish to have offered? What efforts do teachers make to find out "where their students are"? What they are interested in? How do the school's methods and the teachers' methods compare with the media men's methods? Is this a valid comparison?

INVESTIGATE

1 CHOOSE a media man from the past or the present and search out original, primary source material from his or her career to create your own Jackdaw.

2 If you have a local print or broadcast medium that has recently changed management, COMPARE the editorial or program differences before and after the change. If possible, interview the people involved and note how their different policies are reflected in the medium.

3 If you like biography, you might do a comparative study of two men who played decision-making roles in the same medium at the same time; for instance, William Randolph Hearst and Joseph Pulitzer, or David O. Selznick and Louis B. Mayer.

Now that you are on speaking terms with media decision makers, you ought to be ready to do some media marketing of your own. As an advertiser, you must have a keen knowledge of your audiences, your potential consumers. You must know your buyers' needs and create commercial messages that will appeal directly and effectively to the particular audience segment you wish to reach. You must know precisely who this consumer is, how he feels, how he acts. You have the chance to be as wildly creative as Stan Freberg in his Alka-Seltzer ads or as unusual as Binzer, Hurvis, and Churchill in their Screaming Yellow Zonkers campaign.

Here are three ways you can explore the advertising market.

One: How does an advertiser perceive the American youth market? For this, a statement by Pepsi-Cola president, James B. Somerall.

Two: You are the ad agency. How would you create print and radio ads for a product of your choice to be aimed at the teen-age market?

Three: You are the media buyer. What newspapers, what magazines, and what radio stations would you use in order to target your message most effectively to your youth market?

In the Seventies . . .
'You've Got a Lot to Live!'

As seen by James Bentley Somerall,
president, Pepsi-Cola

FEW DECADES have entered the doorway of history as analyzed, heralded, discussed, anticipated and feared as the 1970's.

If almost everyone, everywhere, has awaited this new era with certain apprehension, they've had good reason. Anyone who watched the quiescent fifties turn into the turbulent sixties—with their riots, assassinations, wars, assaults, university take overs, Presidential topplings, pot, and civil strife—might well feel uneasy as another decade arrives.

Many events of the sixties seemed foreign to the way most of us grew up and the values we were taught to respect. But those ways and values could only remain stable if all of us really lived together in a world where they apply. What we learned the hard way in the sixties is that there's a large, restless minority which hasn't been living in the same world with the rest of us; the tumult of the sixties was, in large part, the angry sound of their pounding to be let in.

I'm no seer, nor do I pretend to be a psychologist. I do think, however, the clear message for us in the coming decade—as producers and marketers no less than as citizens—is that we'd better answer the door. Specifically, we'd better prepare effective responses to two major emerging groups whose visible, vocal friendship will be as essential as its lack would be damaging: the young, and the minorities.

Youth of the Seventies

Young people are the orneriest, most critical and questioning, most skeptical and demanding consumer group this country has ever produced. Also the brightest, most socially alive and responsive, most idealistic and relentlessly honest.

The point is that the same snake-cold eye of doubt and scrutiny they direct on all aspects of our society is focused with no less intensity on us who manufacture and offer products aimed at them.

Just as young people are completely unawed by authority in government or educational institutions, quite willing to challenge said credentials, so are they ready to react with open contempt to selling appeals whose authority rests on shaky ground.

Their revenge can be terrible. They may not picket or blow you up, they'll just snicker and turn the other way, leaving you to shout your message into a void.

How do you sell to the young?

Today's youth are perhaps the most formally programed people in history. By the time he reaches the age of 21, it is estimated that a young person has received 15,000 hours of formal instruction through schooling, mostly in the areas of science, arts and humanities.

In the meantime, while receiving these 15,000 hours of formal instruction, he has been exposed to 30,000 hours of television.

It has been seriously advanced by some observers that this 30,000 tv hours is the real education our young people are receiving . . . Their formal education constituting nothing more than an interruption of this process.

To many, television has replaced reading as a pastime. In fact, it can be seriously argued that today's student relies more on tv for his basic information than we did. In many ways, television has become the common denominator of our time.

The tube is King of this generation, much as radio was King to ours.

Much as the young dissenter may deplore the content of mass media . . . and television is beyond question the mass medium of our time . . . the young are in very large measure irretrievably programed as a result of this exposure.

Entirely apart from its content, the penetration of television into every corner of our present existence, its capacity to spew out torrents of data—the meaningful along with the trivial—has shaped the attitudes, ways of comprehending and interacting of our young, far more than the accumulated wisdom of our culture so feebly transmitted in school.

But, naturally, with pictures, instant communication, replay, global transmission, the immediacy and impact are greater. Any advertising that hopes to sell must first communicate with these viewers. It must first be believable . . . on its own terms . . . before it can hope to create acceptance and desire for the product it represents.

In short, advertising better tell the truth. The new idealism and optimism of our kids have turned them away temporarily because of this lack of truth in advertising. But advertising can be good *and* truthful at the same time. The point is to assure both.

Minorities in the Seventies

Here, too, is an area of our society that has undergone volatile changes in the past ten years, but the black man's quest for equality in American society is, hopefully, moving toward its goal.

Every American business today, large or small, is more closely linked to the society as a whole. Meaningful jobs must be made available to a wider pool of labor that includes the black, Puerto Rican, Mexican-American and other minority communities, groups that have long been excluded from the mainstream of commercial life. Even more urgent, we must demonstrate in every visible way our acceptance of them as important participants in the daily life of our country, including their significant role as consumers.

We may still speak of these as minority groups today but the fact is that, in terms of our urban populations, their numbers are concentrated and getting more so. It's been predicted that in the seventies there will be more than 20 American cities with so-called "minority" populations of more than 50 per cent.

Bluntly but most honestly, the conscious or unconscious policies of the white majority have excluded the minorities, now clamoring at last for economic as well as social justice. This is clearly the dominant social pressure of our time and, as such, demands a priority of attention in the seventies.

Pepsi's Got a Lot to Give!

We at Pepsi-Cola Company have started the new decade with a new advertising campaign: "You've Got A Lot To Live! Pepsi's Got A Lot To Give!" This is not by accident. Like many progressive companies in this country, we have kept our eyes and ears open to the nation's changes during the past ten years.

For some years now, we at Pepsi-Cola have conceived and projected to the American public some of the best, most beautiful and most effective advertising in the market.

If we had a formula, it was this: Take America's golden people at play . . . add Pepsi and mix well. We did it in ad after ad. We showed beautiful young people doing beautiful young things.

The strategy couldn't miss: these were the thirst-building activities of the most carefree generation the world has ever seen. The only thing that might have happened to spoil it all would have been if the public had become bored watching all those delicious people having all that fun.

But nobody ever complained to us about seeing those pretty girls . . . and no girl ever asked us to get rid of the good-looking guys. Apparently, nothing could ever go wrong.

Something did.

Overnight it seemed, America simply ran out of giddy young people with nothing on their minds but fun . . . nothing on their faces but grins . . . nothing in their hands but our product.

Overnight, those tanned, frolicsome, "happy-go-lucky" people of the Pepsi Generation began to become advertising anachronisms. They became "square" to the very people we were aiming at.

We weren't "relevant" any more.

Our lily-white "Good-time Charlies" and their dates were coming out of the same tubes that presented a chaotic and ugly reality—death, destruction, corruption and pollution. We had nothing more profound to say than "Drink Up, America."

Many members of Pepsi's historically strongest market segments had turned inward during the sixties. But there are still some things they've kept isolated from bitterness, private things that are pretty hard to lose faith in completely. Things like learning and growing . . . like sharing . . . like loving.

And so, in our new advertising, that's what we talk about, that's what we show, as part of the life of all our people as much a part as our product is. We think this new campaign is right for its time, as much as our old ones were for theirs. We think our new campaign is going to appeal, because it doesn't just sell a product, it sells people. . . .

We hope to sell the greatest country in the world. Not with flags or bunting or patriotic phrases—simply with happiness and love and unquenchable optimism.

We hope to sell the promise that America has never failed to keep—the promise of a good life in a good land, for all those who work at it.

FOCUS

Do you think Somerall gives an accurate
description of youth in the seventies?
Do you agree with his description?

Does Pepsi advertising follow the formula Somerall describes? Is it believable? Is it effective?

Are you aware of any instances of lack
of truth in advertising? Cite specific
examples.

You've got a lot to live. Pepsi's got a lot to give.

LAB YOU ARE THE AD AGENCY

Divide the class into five groups, one each for a specific car, toothpaste, soft drink, hamburger or ice cream chain, pain relief remedy, or some other product of their choice. Pick a specific brand name for the product. Create a new name or use an existing brand. Plan and execute an ad campaign to sell this product to the teen-age market.

First discuss and specify the audience very precisely: who are they? what are their needs? What features of your product precisely meet their needs? What kind of appeal are they likely to respond to? Spend time designing the ad campaign using pictures, headlines, copy, music, and scripted dialogue. Each creative group should then produce a full-page magazine ad and a thirty-second radio commercial for its product.

Here is a description of how Hurvis, Binzer, and Churchill, a young Chicago ad agency, created the campaign for Screaming Yellow Zonkers.

ZONKERS

By Les Bridges

Tho Hurvis, Binzer & Churchill has been creating provocative and sophisticated advertising in Chicago for four and a half years, it had not had a national account until last year. So when Ovaltine Company asked Tom Hurvis, 31, Rollin Binzer, 29, and Mac Churchill, 30, to name, package and create advertising for a new snack, the boys were not about to blow the opportunity. What followed was a crazy name, an outrageous package, hilarious television commercials—and one of the most successful new product introductions in recent grocery marketing history.

The product was Screaming Yellow Zonkers.

How did it come to pass? What seed spawned Screaming Yellow Zonkers? There's someone who can tell us: Rollin Binzer.

Binzer talked softly, pausing to nibble his fingers or fish out another cigaret. "People are sick of advertising. They hate it. Most advertising today treats people like idiots. And people are not idiots." He stopped to hunt for the cigaret pack, then went on. "There are very few products that are worth taking seriously. People don't take products seriously. The only ones that do are the client and the agency. But the world doesn't revolve around a bottle of bleach. If you act as if it does in your advertising, you just turn people off."

Binzer cited the Zonkers campaign to make his point. "Nobody is going to be serious about a box of flavored popcorn that costs 39 cents. Our goal was simply to get people curious enough to try it. So the main part of the campaign was naming the product, and that meant coming up with a name that was so ridiculous that it was intriguing. Names like 'Golden Crunchies' and dumb stuff like that took themselves too seriously. We made a list of about 400 names and the only one anyone could remember was 'Screaming Yellow Zonkers.'"

The idea for putting Zonkers in a black box, something unheard of in the grocery business, came from the client, Ovaltine. Various members of the agency staff contributed the package copy which has become a kind of minor classic. [What Zonkers are made of: Authentic sugar. Absolute popcorn. Honest corn syrup. Vegetable oil with integrity. What Zonkers are lighter than: an anvil, 12 hummingbird wings, three medium-sized trout. ...]

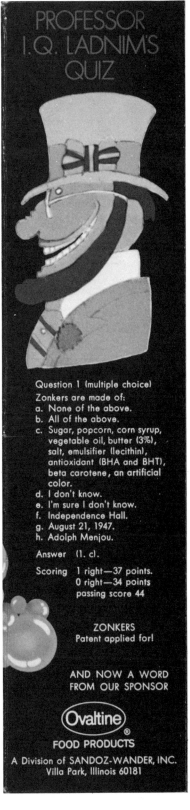

You Are the Ad Agency--Plan Page

Product

Brand Name

Specific Audience

Audience Needs

Theme, Slogan, or Jingle

Graphics

Copy

Music

Voice

Key Selling Point

Display your finished ad or play your taped commercial in class. Question and challenge each other on the effectiveness, specific audience appeal, and interest of each ad.

Does your ad attract attention?

Does it arouse interest in the product?

Does it create the desire to have this particular product?

Is it persuasive enough to produce the actual sale?

Dodge Memo

Select two members of each ad group to be the media buyers. Their task will be to market the campaign that each group has planned. They must place the ads in newspapers and magazines and buy time on various radio stations.

> As the marketplace grows more complex, the advertiser becomes increasingly concerned about delivering his commercials "on target," to the proper person in the proper household.
>
> A. C. NIELSEN COMPANY

What newspapers and magazines will reach your specific intended audience? Which issues will be most effective for sales? How many times do you want to run the ad? What radio stations will give you the strongest reach for your commercial? What time of day will be most effective? How long and how often do you want the spot to go on? What are the costs of magazine space and spot radio time? How will you find out?

Return to the data you collected in the labs on special tastes and special audiences. You will need demographic information from your local broadcasters and publishers. Keep your campaign local. Determine a specific budget for your campaign and stay within it.

As a national advertiser, we must look at all advertising media and determine what balance will bring us the most effective value for each dollar that we spend. We have no set rule that a certain percentage should be spent or will be spent in any medium. We have no requirements to use all media.

It is the job of our advertising department and our agency to decide what combination of media will be best for Dodge. And what is deemed best for cars would be quite different from that which we select for trucks. What was good several years ago or even last year will not determine what we will do now.

Radio has enjoyed many advantages over the years. It has been the timely medium, the "buy now" medium and the medium of wide reach and low production costs.

As we look at radio today we are a bit confused. Even as we have added a variety of models to our car lines, so radio has exploded into many different segments.

FM is reported to have 81% coverage of Detroit homes, plus a vast car audience. In effect the customer now has two complete radio dials to choose from. In Detroit alone there are 13 AM and 18 FM stations.

The new popularity of FM stations with the advent of stereo has diluted the radio buys. What was once a well-defined audience is now split in many ways. Obviously the audience for AM is smaller, but the rates are the same or higher. This is a matter of some concern to us. It takes much more money to get the same impact.

Two basic radio media is only the beginning. Let's remember we are talking about a medium that varies throughout the day. Let's also remember there is a wide, wide variety of radio stations by format. . . .

We wouldn't think of creating a local or regional advertising campaign for our dealer groups without including recommendations for radio. In most cases the combination of newspaper and radio makes the one-two punch that gets local floor traffic and sales. . . .

TV, which is so fine for us nationally, is too expensive for most of our individual dealers. However, our associations balance their campaigns with TV and have had great success with local 10 and 20-second campaigns, but here too the high costs of production and time limit their use of TV.

—R. B. McCurry
general manager
Dodge Car and Truck Division

Print Plan   Radio Plan

The Rating Game which follows is a simulation of the three-way relationship among TV broadcasters, advertisers, and the viewing public who are represented in the audience survey. It is intended to give you a feeling of the dynamics, the competition, and the decision-making processes that are involved in determining what you see and hear on television. You are the decision makers and as such you can choose to be intuitive gamblers, innovative reformers, or cautious readers of the measurement data.

It [the television industry] is not in the business of selling programs to viewers; it is in the business of selling viewers to advertisers. It is a three billion dollar-a-year attention-getting device.   NICHOLAS JOHNSON

The importance of winning the ratings (i.e., beating the competition) is why—to the embarrassment of latter-day executives who want the business to appear more businesslike—television in America resembles a game.

                                                      LES BROWN

How to set up the game:

Divide into three groups, TV networks, advertising agencies, and a rating company. The first group subdivides into three television networks: ABS, NBS, and CBC. In each network certain people should be chosen as president, program director, and sales manager, each with as many staff members as there may be. The second group subdivides into three advertising agencies, designating a company name for each agency. The third group will act as the rating company, will conduct an audience survey, and will calculate which shows are most popular and which networks and agencies make the most profit.

The winners of the game will be the network with the greatest number of ($) points and the agency with the greatest number of ($) points when the television season is finished.

A list of TV shows with brief descriptions, time length, and total cost in number of points is printed on the following pages. One master copy of the list should be cut up and made available for purchasing by the networks.

125 points ($125,000,000) in paper money (or chips or tokens) should be distributed to each of the networks and the same amount to each of the agencies at the beginning of the game. A network pays for half the cost of a show; an agency pays for the other half. As the shows are bought, the money goes into a jackpot to pay the final winners. When the shows are rated and ranked, the network and agency sponsoring each show split evenly the number of points won.

The whole purpose of the [television] enterprise is to hold the attention of the audience long enough for it to be exposed to the commercial. The audience is spoken of in terms of "cost per thousand." NICHOLAS JOHNSON

The game of television is basically between the network and the advertiser, and the Nielsen digits determine what the latter will pay for the circulation of his commercial. The public is involved only as the definition of the number: so many persons 18-49, so many others, all neatly processed by television. LES BROWN

How to play the game:

1   The networks throw a die to determine which one chooses from the list of shows first, second, and last. They keep this order of rotation until all the programs have been bought or until they all run out of ($) points. The networks pay the jackpot for each show they choose to buy (one-half the listed price). These shows are to appear during the opening week of the new season.

In making up their program schedules each network must leave one-half hour prime time open each evening for its affiliates to run local, non-network shows.

BONANZA LAND - Western about a family and its involvement with the problems of other people in the area. Three handsome men star. One hour. 32 points.

BOLD MEN - Series about professionals in their work. Lots of action with well-known stars. One hour. 28 points.

THE CITY - Documentary study of growth problems in urban areas. Includes human interest interviews with city dwellers. One hour. 16 points.

DRUGS AND YOU - Documentary account of drugs and their effects. One hour. 16 points.

FOOTBALL - Exciting pro game. Three hours. 44 points.

FUN-IN - Series of gags and spoofs, quick action, good camera work. One hour. 36 points.

IRONWAYS - Police officer who solves crimes with shrewd insight and deduction. Lots of action from younger helpers. One hour. 30 points.

THE LUCY HOUR - Famous comedienne does her own show with lots of laughs and slapstick humor. Guest stars appear. One hour. 26 points.

MISSION: ACTION - Spy thriller in which a team of experts foils enemy plots with superb technology. One hour. 30 points.

NEWS WITH DAN AND DICK - Well-known news commentators with large following. Somewhat liberal in their commentaries. One-half hour. 14 points.

NEWS WITH CRICKITE - Perceptive reporter and analyst with good following. One-half hour. 14 points.

TEAM NEWS - Group of newsmen, young and new to the public, offer colorful features and much human interest. One-half hour. 14 points.

NIGHT MOVIE - 1960's movies with lots of action and heavy drama. Two hours. 30 points. (Name the movie)

MOVIELAND - Movies of the '30's in the style of Bogart. Rough and ready. Two hours. 26 points.

MOON WALK - Actual film clips and footage from latest moon landing. Two hours. 38 points.

NETWORK MOVIE NIGHT - Made-for-TV movie about a man and a woman in neighboring apartments. Comedy with lots of laughs. Two hours. 28 points.

MOD CREW - Teen-age police group work to help kids and solve crimes. Fast action, strong teen identification with the good guys. One hour. 36 points.

OLYMPIC FINALS - Soccer, track, and swimming finals carried live by satellite. One hour. 40 points.

SCHOOL EXPLOSION - Report on what is happening in education across the country. Documents some exciting new developments. One hour. 14 points.

TO LOVE FROM ROME - Short sketches of life and love in Rome. One hour. 14 points.

TWILIGHT TIME - Series of mystery stories and stranger-than-fiction tales of suspense. One-half hour. 16 points.

PREMIER MOVIE - Made-for-TV movie, a suspense and intrigue plot, could become a series. One and one-half hours. 24 points.

HOMBRE - Western with smiling hero who tries to avoid all dangerous situations except women. When forced into danger he usually talks his way out of it. One-half hour. 14 points.

O'MALLEY, TREASURY AGENT - The agent methodically tracks down smugglers and income tax evaders. One hour. 22 points.

CONNOLLEY - Police investigator solves homicides and robberies using his efficient staff and police procedures. One hour. 20 points.

ALL CALL - Two patrolmen on the beat with human interest incidents in a policeman's day. One hour. 12 points.

BLIND MAN'S BLUFF - Blind private investigator solves crimes by using his heightened senses of hearing, smelling, and intuition. One hour. 24 points.

HOSPITAL - Focuses on two doctors who handle medical problems and the psychological upsets that frequently accompany them. One is a kindly fatherly type doctor and the other is young, handsome, and impetuous. One hour. 28 points.

CINDY - Top film star in light situation comedy of her own. One-half hour. 16 points.

THE JOHNNY APPLE SHOW - Famous country and western singer heads show with guest stars. One hour. 28 points.

THEATER SPECIAL - Dramatic play with two well-known broadway stars in a special showing of new play. One and one-half hour. 32 points.

2   When the program schedules for three nights have been set up by each of the networks, their sales managers offer the schedules of shows to the advertising agencies to bid on. The agencies throw a die to determine the order in which they bid. The network salesmen should try to persuade the agency buyers to buy their programs because of the promise of good ratings, the popularity of similar shows, the strong position in the schedule, the weakness of the competition. The buying continues in rotation until all the shows have been bought or until the agencies use up all their ($) points. The agencies pay (the jackpot) half the point value of each show they buy.

If any shows scheduled by the networks are not bought by the agencies, the network may borrow money from the jackpot to underwrite the entire show, or they can withdraw it, reclaim two-thirds of their cost from the jackpot, and use the money in the "second season."

3   When the schedules are set and the shows are sold to advertisers, the Rating Company (RC) runs an audience survey to determine the most popular shows.

Members of the RC must determine a plan for the audience survey which will represent an actual cross section of the TV audience. The demographic categories on page 50 should be helpful.

When the network schedule is complete, the RC duplicates the schedule with brief show descriptions for each night. This will be a TV viewing guide. The RC also prepares and duplicates a three-night viewing diary modeled after the form which appears below.

Each person in the survey is asked to fill out a diary for three nights, selecting which shows he would watch at each viewing time. Only one show can be checked at the same time slot. If he would not watch any of the programs offered, he leaves the diary unmarked at that time.

Sunday	ABS	NBS	CBC
6:00			
6:30			
7:00			
7:30			
8:00			
8:30			
9:00			
9:30			

Monday	ABS	NBS	CBC
6:00			
6:30			
7:00			
7:30			
8:00			
8:30			
9:00			
9:30			

Tuesday	ABS	NBS	CBC
6:00			
6:30			
7:00			
7:30			
8:00			
8:30			
9:00			
9:30			

4   After the audience survey is taken, the RC compiles the data from the diaries and assigns the percentage of the total viewing audience to each show. Based on this percentage the shows should be ranked from highest to lowest. The top show wins 50 points, the next 48, and so on, each place dropping two points. (If several shows tie with the same percentage, they all hold the same value, but the next show drops two points for every show involved in the tie.)

Example: The sampling is made up of 40 people, 100 percent of the possible viewing audience. On Monday at 8 p.m., the "Johnny Apple Show" had 10 viewers or 25 percent; "Bold Men" had 12 viewers or 30 percent; and Pro Football had 14 viewers or 33 percent of the possible viewing audience. Four persons in the sampling checked none of the offerings.

If an hour or two-hour or three-hour program has different percentages at each half-hour breakdown, the program gets credit for the highest percentage it receives.

When all the percentages are worked out for the twenty-four time slots each night, the top shows get 50 points. The 33 percent watching Pro Football may turn out to be in fifth placed tied with two others and, as such, is worth 40 points [50 - (2 x 5)]. The next show at 31 percent would then drop to eighth place because of the tie and would win 36 points.

5   Networks and agencies split the winnings on each show based on the RC ratings.

6   At this point each network and each agency throw a die and follow the instructions listed below under the number that they roll. If a network or an agency throws a number already thrown, they throw again until they throw a new number.

Networks

1 The President asks for an hour of prime time to discuss a national crisis. Your top-rated show is preempted. Pay the jackpot 5 points.

2 Midway through the first showing of a prime-series you have network video trouble. Pay the jackpot 3 points.

3 Your network has more affiliates than all of your competitors. Collect 15 points from the jackpot.

4 Your network did an outstanding pre-season promotional job. Collect 20 points from the jackpot.

5 Some of your affiliates reject some of your programming in favor of local revenue shows. Pay the jackpot 8 points.

6 You failed to pilot three of your new shows for possible revision. Pay the jackpot 5 points.

Agencies

1 One of your major shows receives bad pre-season reviews. Pay the jackpot 5 points.

2 Weekend slotting for one of your prime advertisers fails to capture young adult audience he wanted. Pay the jackpot 3 points.

3 Style of show matches the style of your commercials--both catch on. Collect 15 points from the jackpot.

4 The star of your major show is picked up at a pot party with sensational press coverage. Collect 3 points from jackpot.

5 Your show follows one that is a complete bust. You lose many viewers who "tune" to other networks. Pay 4 points to the jackpot.

6 Revision of show title and format based on preview reactions produces a winner. Collect 10 points from the jackpot.

7 After the networks and agencies have finished the first season and claimed their returns, the networks may adjust their program schedules for the second season. They discuss these changes with the agency salesmen. If a network and agency decide to drop a show, they each pay the jackpot two points. A new show which a network can prepare and sell to an agency costs 30 points.

All sports, specials, and documentaries should be redescribed for the second season. Networks and agencies will again pay the jackpot for the programs in the second season.

8 With the new schedule and revised descriptions, the RC takes a second season survey as it did before with the diaries. They calculate the ratings again and announce the top programs.

The winning network and the winning agency are the ones with the most ($) points at the end of the second season. Have fun!

How do you account for your winning or losing in the Rating Game?

Do you think the sampling used by the Rating Company was representative of the general American public?

If you owned every show on the list, do you think you could set up the perfect network schedule for three evenings for the audience in your sampling? If so, what would it look like?

Do you see any ways in which this system does not reflect or correspond to popular tastes?

In what ways did the results of the Rating Game support the conclusions you had drawn from earlier labs? Or did these results force you to modify your earlier conclusions?

INTERFACE

Take several TV shows that you like and that do not have top ratings. See whether you can revise their evening schedules so that these shows will have improved ratings and stand a better chance of re-appearing next season.

Twice a year at Christmas and in the spring the rating companies do not publish results of their surveys. These weeks are known as "blackouts" in the industry. Check the programming during these "blackouts" to see if there are any changes and if so, what these changes are. How would you account for such changes?

Have you ever been critical of the "Rating Game" method of keeping or dropping TV shows? If so, did you find yourself ignoring the chance to make points in the game in order to schedule or sponsor programs you thought deserved to be scheduled? Do you think a person's real values can be submerged in a simulation, or in the excitement of the game does the "self" that always wants to win come out on top?

INVESTIGATE

1 INTERVIEW the personnel of a local advertising agency to discover how they use ratings to place TV spots during prime time broadcasting.

2 INVESTIGATE new FCC rulings about the proportion of local broadcasting, public service broadcasting, and non-network broadcasting necessary for renewal of local licenses.

3 INTERVIEW regional TV station managers about their network's plotting of the season's schedule in terms of the geographic audience this station broadcases for.

Where I Stand -

Based on your experience with the units in this section, which of the following positions seems better to you?

a) I believe that publishers and broadcasters should make audience surveys to identify popular tastes, popular thresholds, and the public's needs. They should then produce publications and programs accordingly.	b) I believe that individual members of society should be exposed to a wide variety of media offerings and should learn to make choices that will meet their individual needs, tastes, and thresholds.

SIMULATE

Using the insights and conclusions you arrived at above, role play the following Media Man Simulation.

You are the program director of a major television network. You have been offered a dramatic series modeled after the investigations of consumer advocate Ralph Nader. You feel that the time is ripe for such a program, although you know it will be difficult to find sponsors for the show. In the past your network has failed with such "relevant" shows. But the scripts and casts are excellent. Will you program the show? How will you decide? How will you explain your decision to network officials?

Everybody experiences far more than he understands. Yet it is experience, far more than understanding, that influences behavior, especially in collective matters of media and technology, where the individual is almost inevitably unaware of their effect upon him. MARSHALL MCLUHAN

The daily journal is like the mirror—it reflects that which is before it. . . . Let those who are startled by it blame the people who are before the mirror, and not the mirror, which only reflects their features and actions.

JOSEPH PULITZER

Broadcasting is many different things, but above all it is the act of creating images. At first through sound alone, and later through the combination of sound, sight and motion, it has been implanting images in the minds of multitudes of people for more than three decades—images of themselves and the objective world in which they live, as well as images of their aspirations, of the kind of world in which they would like to live. CBS TELEVISION NETWORK

The Media Image and Massage

There is widespread public concern about the influence television has on its viewers, especially the influence of TV violence on the young. Critics point to the rising crime rate insisting it is the result of the constant barrage of fights, shootings, and frauds acted out hourly on the screen. The following lab attempts to reveal how television may or may not have influenced your ways of thinking.

 THE MEDIA "RORSCHACH" TEST

There are ten exercises in this lab; each one gives you the beginning of an incident, then four possible solutions. In Part I you are to choose the solution which you think would make the best TV drama. Record your choice in the proper space on page 93.

1 A U.S. scientist with information about a new nuclear weapon has been kidnapped by a small foreign country. A group has been assigned to recapture him before he tells the secret. They . . .

  a infiltrate the home of the dictator as servants and handymen and by playing on jealousies contrive to have the dictator and his right-hand man kill each other. The group escapes with the scientist.

  b persuade the dictator to accept ransom money for the scientist by showing him all the economic benefits he can gain from the money and promised technical aid.

  c work closely with an international police organization and intercept the kidnappers with the scientist at the airport through much cooperation.

  d find that the scientist had not been kidnapped but had withdrawn to this small country to farm so that he would not have to use his knowledge to destroy.

2   A street gang youth has been shot, apparently by a rival gang. The case is resolved by . . .

   a   a group of undercover police who pose as members of the dead boy's gang. There is a shoot out in which several people are wounded but the rival gang members are arrested.

   b   a group of police who cover the neighborhood asking everyone in the vicinity for information. Through a long, tedious process the gang members are identified and arrested to await trial.

   c   a band of local businessmen who offer a reward for information leading to the arrest of the killers. The reward prompts quick action in the neighborhood.

   d   his father, who investigates the case. The mother is extremely upset over the situation and fears for the lives of the other children. The father finally stops his search and moves the whole family out of the city.

3   A doctor has a patient who is about to die from cancer. He . . .

   a   asks the patient's permission to do research on the disease. Although the patient will die, the knowledge gained will help others in the near future.

   b   administers a lethal drug because of the severe pain faced by the patient and the inevitability of death.

   c   advises the patient to enjoy a beach vacation. The patient doesn't know his condition and does not have to face it.

   d   discovers that the wealthy patient has bribed an orderly with $10,000 to steal some narcotics with which he ends his life.

4   A group of young people want to draw attention to a local politician's graft which they have discovered. They . . .

   a   carefully instruct other students in the facts of the case and organize a sizable house-to-house doorbell campaign to inform the voters.

   b   stage a sit-in in the politician's office to publicize their findings. The mayor orders the police to forcibly remove them. The press interviews the students.

   c   organize a boycott of companies that were benefiting from the good "services" of the politician.

   d   are convinced by the politician that these methods were necessary for him in order to achieve some other very worthwhile goals.

5 A teacher is faced with two groups in her class who dislike each other intensely. The teacher . . .

   a gets the leaders of the groups to lead a series of informal discussions on films and novels. The two groups find they have much in common and become friendly.

   b largely ignores the situation until a knife fight breaks out in the classroom and one boy is wounded.

   c jokes with other teachers about the situation and it remains the same. The students do enough class work to get by and pass the course.

   d asks the head of a large company that hires many of these students to fund a counselling staff. The president agrees, and the teacher is able to cope with the situation with the added staff.

6 A soldier just assigned to overseas duty meets and falls in love with a girl. They have known each other for four weeks. He . . .

   a writes to the girl for a year. After that the girl marries someone else and he returns home to marry another girl he has known since grade school.

   b marries the girl, goes overseas, and is killed in battle. The soldier's best buddy returns home to tell the wife of her husband's death as a hero. She then falls in love with him.

   c marries the girl but when he returns home with psychological problems from shell shock, he finds that she gets on his nerves. He plots to kill her but is stopped in the act by her brother.

   d can't get married because neither of them has enough money. When his company learns about this, they all chip into a kitty so that the couple can get married.

7 A businessman goes deeply into debt and has to pay a group of creditors who are threatening him. He . . .

   a finds a loan shark who lends him the money but later threatens his life if he doesn't cooperate in certain unsavory deals.

   b goes bankrupt and starts his life over again in another city. Although he never regains his former wealth, he's happy to be relieved of the pressure.

   c arranges financing through an old friend who is vice-president of a bank. He works for ten years to repay the debt.

   d contacts an insurance friend who calls the creditors together and convinces them that they will profit more by working with the businessman and extending his credit.

8   Two young men, Cal and Jim, leave home and school to find out what the world's all about. Jim gets into hard drugs several weeks after they start their travels. Cal . . .

a   follows Jim's motorcycle one evening to confront the pusher and cut off the drugs before his friend is hooked. But Jim spots Cal and opens up a high-speed chase. The police join the chase, the speed increases and the chase ends in a blinding crash against a highway abutment. Jim is permanently paralyzed.

b   learns about a halfway house for addicts and draws Jim into the group. At first his friend resists but then he becomes attracted to a girl there in worse straits than he is. Jim stays and accepts help.

c   talks to Jim's rich uncle and finally convinces him that he should try to help. The uncle underwrites methodone research in a nearby hospital with the understanding that the research director will try to help his nephew.

d   decides to try to find out what caused his friend to turn to drugs. He discovers a letter from a girl friend accusing Jim of going on the trip to get away from his inability to make decisions about his future. Cal calls the girl, convinces the two that they must talk it out. But weakened by the drugs and afraid of a confrontation, Jim disappears before the girl arrives.

9   An ex-convict named Jeff moves into a neighborhood with his wife and two children. He conceals his past and . . .

a   joins a club organized to help the neighborhood youth. One boy in the club is a petty thief and will accept no counseling; Jeff decides to reveal his experiences to the boy in order to help him. The boy threatens to reveal the information but finally comes to respect Jeff. So do the other boys in the club. In a special award dinner Jeff reveals his past to the whole group.

b   discovers a fellow worker who knows of his past. The worker threatens to blackmail Jeff. They fight on a construction site and the potential blackmailer strikes his head and dies. Jeff flees the scene, gets drunk, and joins an armed robbery plot. As he leaves with the robbers, you learn that the worker's death has been ruled accidental.

c   struggles to make ends meet. His new home is in a strange city away from his former friends. When a former cell mate appears, Jeff agrees to help the man financially if he'll leave. The man finally leaves, and Jeff discovers he's in line for a promotion.

d   thinks everything is finally working out. He doesn't know that his wife has intercepted mail from his former gang. One of the gang finally comes to the house and finds the wife alone. She stands up to him, and he agrees to leave without talking to Jeff. But Jeff is ashamed and angry when he discovers the intercepted mail and the risks his wife has taken. He cannot face the humiliation and leaves quietly one night.

10 A stranger appears in a western town, begins gambling, and wins heavily the first night. He's accused of cheating and . . .

  a a fight breaks out. The sheriff stops the fight and orders the stranger to leave town. The stranger leaves but returns secretly to get revenge on the man who accused him of cheating. He discovers that the man is married to his former sweetheart, so he stops short of his intended murder and leaves town suddenly.

  b is badly beaten by those who lost money in the game. When he later goes to report the foul play, he's ambushed, a shoot out ensues, and he's wounded but kills his three attackers.

  c returns his winnings rather than risk being killed by the angry losers. When the local marshall learns of the incident, he offers him a job as deputy marshall. As such the stranger arrests the man who accused him of cheating. The charge: swindling poor ranchers in the area.

  d challenges his opponents to an all-or-nothing game. He puts all his winnings on the line. The game is very tense. The stranger has a weak hand. He cannot pull out because his winnings are already committed. So he boldly doubles the stakes. His opponents fold. He wins.

Place your responses to the choice that would make the best television show below:

1_____   3_____   5_____   7_____   9_____

2_____   4_____   6_____   8_____   10_____

Part II

Now read each of the situations again and choose a solution based on the way you think you would want the problem solved if you were personally involved, if you were faced with the same problem. Write in your choice below. If none of the possibilities satisfy you, write "none."

1_____   3_____   5_____   7_____   9_____

2_____   4_____   6_____   8_____   10_____

Now check the scoring sheet in the Teacher's Guide for an interpretation of your responses. Do a tally of your responses below.

Type of Solutions	Best TV Show Choices	Personal Involvement Choices
Type One		
Type Two		
Type Three		
Type Four		

What was the predominant type of solution
you chose for the best TV show? Can you
explain this pattern in your choices?

What was the predominant type of solution
you chose for real-life situations in which
you might be personally involved? Can you
explain this pattern in your choices?

Are your expectations about what type of
behavior will make a good TV show the
same as the type of behavior you value
and prize in your day-to-day living?

What is the correlation between your choices
for TV drama and your choices for real-life
situations in which you might be personally
involved?
High correlation?   Low correlation?

How do you interpret the high or low correlation of your choice for good TV drama
and for real-life situations?

In the class as a whole was the correlation
high or low between good TV drama choices
and real-life personal involvement choices?

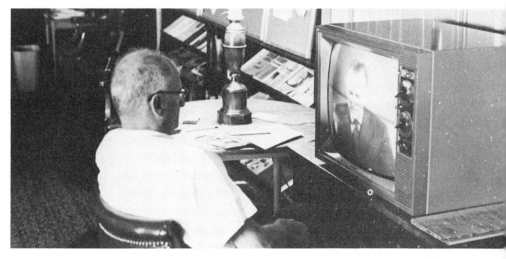

INTERFACE

Television shows and commercials often offer instant solutions to complicated problems. Do you sense an impatience in yourself in dealing with long drawn out procedures to solving problems that might be due to the influence of television?

Review some of the latest jargon and popular expressions used by your peers. Did any of it originate in the mass media, or has any of it been popularized by the mass media?

Teens and twenty-year-olds who were heavily imprinted with television as infants show a strong degree of involvement with national issues. Yet voting officials are already complaining about the low degree of interest in voter registration since the passage of the 18-year-old vote. Do any of the results of the Media Rorschach test help you explain this apparent contradiction?

Do you think the current use of drugs has been influenced by the thousands of pill commercials young people have viewed since early childhood?

INVESTIGATE

1   STUDY the report of the National Commission on the Causes and Prevention of Violence for its observations on the media.

2   INVESTIGATE the incidents leading up to the establishment of the Hays Office in the 1930's to control crime and violence in motion pictures. Compare its history to the Pastore Senate Committee on TV violence.

3   The Surgeon General's Office published its report on the correlations between violence on TV and violence in the nation's children in January, 1972. Investigate reviews of the report in the New York Times, the National Observer, Newsweek, and other periodicals. Do the Surgeon General's findings agree with the results of your lab?

The complex interaction between the media and culture makes them almost inseparable. Yet media can tell us a great deal about the culture of any age. Like the tombs of the Pharoahs of Egypt, which give us glimpses of what that society was like, contemporary media will give future generations a picture of our society. But how accurate will the picture be?

LAB AMERICAN DIG

To look at the interaction between contemporary media and culture it is important to try to be a detached observer. It is the year 2284. You are a group of archeologists from the planet X-917 who are trying to discover the patterns of society in the United States, Earth during the 1970's. Like archeologists of all ages you will have to discover the culture of the people you are studying by examining the artifacts they have left behind. The only remaining indications of that society is the group of magazine covers on the following pages. Answer the following questions about that society and base your answers ONLY on the magazine covers.

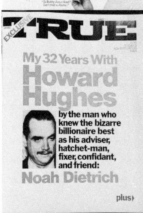

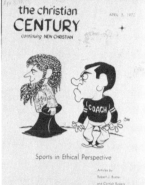

Physical characteristics of the people:

Color   Size

Complexion   Standard of physical beauty

Health   Diet

Communication patterns:

Language   Education

Dress   Literature

Drama

Socio-Economic patterns:

Class structure   Occupations/job roles

Agrarian/industrial/mixed economy Leisure-time pursuits

Means of distribution   Housing

Standard of living   Transportation

Religious values and practices:

God(s)   Good/evil

Rituals   Moral laws

Afterlife   Religious leaders

Political structures:

Type of government   Loyalty of citizens

Law and order   Stability of political life

System of justice   Opportunity for dissent

Compile a class list of inferences and observations which you were able to make about American society in 1972 from the magazine covers which you examined.

What predominant patterns emerge?

Are there important areas of American life that were not represented by the magazine covers? How would you account for this?

LAB TIME CAPSULE

Most major public buildings have a cornerstone indicating the date the building was erected. Inside some of the cornerstones there is a time capsule, a sealed box containing items of contemporary interest for historical record. If and when the building is torn down, the time capsule will yield a unique glimpse into the ideas and values, the culture and events of the times.

The public library building in one of our major cities was built in 1915. According to library documents, the time capsule contains:

a letters from President Woodrow Wilson, the governor, and the mayor

b the city newspapers for the date of the cornerstone laying

c a copy of the Bible and the American flag

d copies of the architect's drawings for the library building

e a record of all the library employees with a commentary by the head librarian

f pictures and drawings of the city

g a record of major contributors to the building

h the cornerstone dedication address delivered by the president of Harvard College

i a World War I infantryman's helmet

j a secret box containing "items of interest to posterity"

Your city is in the process of planning a new city hall. You have been chosen to assemble materials for a time capsule which will be sealed in the foundation of the building and which is supposed to reflect as accurately as possible today's American culture. The city council requests that all the contents of the capsule be samples of the mass media today. Space will allow for the following items, you specify the contents. Discuss each choice, and insofar as possible, assemble the items, bring them into class, and indicate the significance of each one.

2 newspapers

_____

_____

3 books

_____

_____

_____

1 hour of radio programming on tape

Stations: ____ ____ ____ ____

Programs:

_____

_____

_____

_____

3 hours of videotape

Programs:

_____

_____

_____

5 magazines

_____

_____

_____

_____

_____

2 movies

_____

_____

10 records

_____

_____

_____

_____

_____

_____

_____

Do the media allowed by the Time Capsule
lab give you enough opportunity to present
a fairly accurate view of American society?

Are there any groups in America today
who would have to prepare items vastly different from yours in order to give a picture
of the way they see American society?

Are there any fairly common media products
you would definitely not include in the time
capsule?

Marshall McLuhan has said, "Ads are the cave art of the twentieth century." Ads reveal some of the deepest values in our culture. Select a task force to create a collage of ads from magazines, newspapers, or photos of TV commercials (1/15 second, wide open) that will reflect as accurately as possible the image of America today.

INTERFACE

Can you think of any characters in television, film, magazines, or books that give a fairly accurate picture of the way you live?

What came first, the counter culture and the youth cult or the labels put on them by the media? Is there such a phenomenon as the youth culture?

Does any of the nostalgia craze, reprints of old catalogs and releases of early movies, relate to a need for the media-mirror function we have examined here?

INVESTIGATE

1 DID Shakespeare present an accurate image of 17th century England in his plays?

2 Time magazine has published several time-capsule books. Take the one for 1945 and ASK your parents or relatives about how well Time presented the world they knew at that time.

3 FIND OUT what items are enclosed in the foundation of your school and/or local public buildings.

4 EXAMINE the rise of minority group magazines and newspapers. What prompted their emergence?

The historians and archeologists will one day discover that the ads of our times are the richest and most faithful daily reflections that any society ever made of its entire range of activities.   MARSHALL MCLUHAN

The motion pictures present our customs and our daily life more distinctly than any other medium and, therefore, if we were to come back a thousand years from today and tried to find some form of expression that would more clearly, more perfectly explain how we live today, it would have to be the motion picture, because there is no medium of today that so universally must please as great a number of people.   IRVING THALBERG

It is certainly true that newspapers affect public opinion, but a process point of view argues that it is equally true that public opinion affects the newspapers.   DAVID BERLO

Where I Stand -	Based on your experience with the units in this section, which of the following positions seems better to you?
a) I believe that my thinking and my behavior are strongly influenced by the mass media. Because of this dramatic impact, I believe that some controls on the media are necessary to insure that they do not misrepresent our culture or become a destructive influence on the behavior of citizens.	b) I believe that the mass media is only one among many influences on my thinking and behavior. I am personally responsible and can evaluate that influence. I can live agreeably in a society which does not place controls on its media.

SIMULATE

Using the insights and conclusions you arrived at above, role play the following Media Man Simulation.

You are the managing editor of a national photo-weekly magazine. You have four front cover photo possibilities to highlight your feature article on women's liberation. One photo is a close-up of a woman in heated debate, mouth open. A second shows a protest sign in the foreground with the Miss America promenade in the background. A third shows dishes in the sink as a woman dressed for work shuts the door behind her. A fourth is an imaginative cheesecake shot of a beautiful young woman in astronaut gear. Which one will you use and why?

the news
media

People live by what they know. They make decisions on the basis of their knowledge. The quality of their information is critical to the quality of their lives.

One of the major services of the mass media is to provide information. The news itself, then, is of primary importance in all the mass media; the quality of the news is critically important to the quality of life in a democratic society.

The second part of this program sets out a series of lab experiments and inquiries designed to explore the people's need for news, the ways in which the news is gathered, and the decision-making processes which determine what we see and hear via the different news media.

The basis of our government being the opinion of the people, the very first object should be to keep that right; and were it left to me to decide whether we should have a government without newspapers, or newspapers without government, I should not hesitate to prefer the latter.

THOMAS JEFFERSON

In its most common role, as a follower and repackager of news stories, a headline service for busy people, TV news has done admirably. . . . Its greatest triumphs have been as slice-of-life dramatist, at those times when it has made the viewer an eye-witness to history.

But the final test of television as a medium of journalism doesn't depend on its success as a "look here, folks" machine. The true test is whether it has told society what it needs to know in order to make intelligent decisions about itself. Whether it has told the truth.

RICHARD TOWNLEY

The People's Need to Know

PROBE

How does the quality of man's knowledge
affect the quality of his life?

The lab which follows introduces a way of probing the relationship between a man's knowledge and his life by proposing a situation in which one depends immediately upon the other.

 SPACED-OUT

You are one of the crew of a space ship originally scheduled to rendezvous with a mother ship on the lighted surface of the moon. Due to mechanical problems your ship was forced to land at a spot some two hundred miles from the rendezvous point. During the approach and landing much of the equipment aboard your ship was damaged. Your survival now depends upon your reaching the mother ship two hundred miles away. It is critical that you make wise choices in selecting just what equipment you can carry and what will be absolutely necessary for reaching the mother ship. What is less necessary must be left behind.

Part 1

Your task is to check over the list of remaining supplies and rank them in order of importance for your survival on the trip to the mother ship. Place the number 1 next to the most important item, number 2 for the next most important, and so on through number 15, the least important.

_____ Box of matches
_____ Food concentrate
_____ 50 feet of nylon rope
_____ Parachute silk
_____ Portable heating unit
_____ Two .45 caliber pistols
_____ One case dehydrated milk
_____ Two 100 pound tanks of oxygen
_____ Stellar map, of stars visible from the moon
_____ Life raft
_____ Magnetic compass
_____ 5 gallons of water
_____ Signal flares
_____ First-aid kit containing injection needles
_____ Solar-powered FM receiver-transmitter

Part 2

Now join five other members of the class to form a space crew. Be sure to include at least one crew member who is knowledgeable in chemistry and physics. After listening to the choices each crew member made about the importance of each item for survival, try to arrive at a group consensus on the priorities.

Use the grid on this page to list your own selection of priorities and your crew's consensus. Finally check the Mass Media Teacher's Guide for the priorities set up by the National Aeronautics and Space Administration (NASA) and add this information to the grid. The NASA priorities, of course, are derived from the knowledge and experience of their specialists.

	My Priorities	My Crew's Priorities	NASA's Priorities
Box of matches			
Food concentrate			
50 feet of nylon rope			
Parachute silk			
Portable heating unit			
Two .45 caliber pistols			
One case dehydrated milk			
Two 100 pound tanks of oxygen			
Stellar map of stars visible from the moon			
Life raft			
Magnetic compass			
5 gallons of water			
Signal flares			
First-aid kit containing injection needles			
Solar-powered FM receiver-transmitter			

Assuming that NASA's information and priorities are the most reliable, would you have survived if your information alone had been used to make decisions for the crew?

Assuming NASA's information and priorities most reliable, what would your crew's chances have been relying on their own consensus?

If you have someone in your class generally recognized as knowledgeable in natural sciences, ask the student to read and account for his original choices. What would the crew's chances of survival have been acting on his priorities?

Because your lives depended on the quality and accuracy of your information, did you find your crew questioning or challenging the reliability of the information you had at your disposal for decision making?

Did individuals or crews change their priorities and decisions because new information was introduced, information not previously known?

INTERFACE

Reflect on your own personal life (here on earth) and note below instances in which you receive news/information from the mass media which more or less immediately affect your personal decision making.

News/information   Decisions

Do you ever evaluate the news/information you receive in the media as critically or thoroughly as you evaluated information as a member of the space crew?

You are the first high school generation presented with the power to affect political life in American society through the 18-year-old vote. Has this changed your attitude or that of your classmates about the need for information about politics and government?

Certain studies have indicated that youth in the seventies are "turned off" by the news media. Do you think this is true? If it is, what effect will this have on society in general?

Rumors and gossip are usually the fasting moving news items on any campus. How many decisions have you made in the past week based on this type of information? Which ones would you remake if you had the chance? Why?

In the event of a crisis in school, a fire or a bomb threat, who's directions or information would you accept?

In 1971 CBS began broadcasting special newscasts for seven to eleven-year-olds during the Saturday cartoons. What do you think of this idea? Should there be special newscasts for twelve to seventeen-year-olds? Is the quality of news/information as important for the life of a child or a teen-ager as it is for the life of an adult?

INVESTIGATE

1   LOOK UP the story of the famous "War of the Worlds" radio broadcast in 1938. Because many who tuned into the drama thought they were listening to an authentic news report about an invasion from Mars, the broadcast triggered many frantic "life-saving" decisions. Several studies are available; so is a record of the original broadcast.

2   SECURE a copy of the film "Case History of a Rumor" available through B'nai Brith film libraries. This CBS documentary was never shown on network television because officials were afraid listeners might make a "War of the Worlds" reaction if they tuned in after the broadcast had begun. Judge the quality of decisions based on rumored information.

3   The Spanish-American War has often been referred to as a war caused by "Yellow Journalism." The label "Yellow Journalism" grew out of the practice by William Randolph Hearst to print part of his paper, especially comic strips, on yellow paper. His paper and Joseph Pulitzer's newspaper conducted an intense battle to win the largest circulation in New York City. Sensational news was vital to this battle, especially with semi-literate emigrant readers; Hearst and Pulitzer were charged with capitalizing on the Cuban problem in order to create sensational news. Investigate this charge thoroughly, don't accept generalizations. Did the public accept untruths that led the nation into war?

The space lab explored the relationship between man's knowledge and his life, in ultimate circumstances. The following lab proposes to examine the same relationship in the less critical, but nevertheless important circumstances of your own day-to-day life here on earth.

LAB   PERSONAL NEWS INVENTORY

Part 1   Make a list of the various roles and responsibilities you now have. Then consider what information you regularly need in each of these roles in order to perform well, in order to protect yourself, in order to make decisions. Where do you get that information?

Role responsibility	Information needed	Information sources
Member of school community		
Member of family		
Member of peer group		
Member of civic community		
Employee		

Driver, commuter, traveler		
Consumer of products		
Seeker of entertainment		
Other		

Take any one of the sources you listed above that represent a form of the mass media (newspaper, magazine, books, radio, TV) and estimate as best you can what time, money, experience, and contacts you would need to get this same information yourself if the medium did not exist.

Information needed:

Information source:

Time needed to acquire information my-self:

Money needed to acquire information my-self:

Experience needed to acquire and inter-pret information accurately:

Contacts needed to get the information:

On the basis of the time, money, experience, and contacts needed to acquire this in-formation, how well could you satisfy your information/news needs without the help of the professional information services?

Part 2 Review your last 24 hours and briefly summarize the NEW information you
have acquired in that time. Then make a check in the appropriate column below whether
you sought the information, or it "found" you, and whether your source was the news
media or some other source of information.

NEW information	I sought the info.	Info. "found" me	Source	
			News Media	Other
Last Night's game scores	✔		✔	
Injury of a friend		✔		✔
Totals:				

What percent of your new information do
you get from the news media each day?

If possible, calculate a class average of
how much new information you receive
from the news media each day?

Was the class average similar to your
own percentage figure? If not, can you
explain the difference?

Part 3   Review your own use of the news media and note the sources and times below.

News Media	Time of Day	Usual amount of time with this source	Available:		
			Daily	Weekly	Monthly

Based on the data compiled above, would you consider your news experience as

__ Random and unpredictable
__ Fairly consistent
__ Habitual, rarely varies

Does this picture satisfy you?

Would you like to change it in any way?

Is money or time a factor?

INTERFACE

When did you actually read a newspaper or listen to a news broadcast for the first time? Can you remember? How has your use of the news media changed since that time? Do you find children today entering into the news media experience the way you began?

Do groups of students congregate at certain times and certain places in the school building as a way of exchanging information, even if they don't consciously realize that they are fulfilling that purpose? If so, how does this exchange of information differ from the school's news media in a) frequency b) immediacy c) interest d) reliability e) diversity of information f) availability of information.

INVESTIGATE

1   INTERVIEW a person in your community who has fairly heavy social or professional responsibilities. Inquire about his use of the news media. What regular patterns does he have? Compare these to your own and the class's patterns of news media use.

2   TALK to some children who do not as yet use news media but who can speak and listen, perhaps even read. Ask them about persons or events whose existence has been largely made known by the news media. If they have answers, attempt to find out their information sources.

Where I Stand - Based on your experience with the units in this section, which of the following positions seems better to you?	
a) The processes of personal information gathering are generally very casual and unplanned. I will normally just have to hope for the best when I am faced with an unexpected decision.	b) Education in our society teaches us information-gathering skills so that we can acquire the information we need to make responsible decisions. I expect to be prepared to cope with most unexpected decisions.

The Professional Newsman

The test of a good newspaperman's work is simply stated, and massively difficult to achieve, and it is this: in his role as a stand-in for those who are not able to see the event, does his reportage enable them to reach the same general impression that the event itself would give them?

ROGER TATARIAN

[The newspaper reporter] does not owe primary allegiance to the owner of his newspaper, or to his managing editor, or to his government, or to the sources of his information: he owes it to the people. JAMES RESTON

Examining substance in the daily press or on the air reveals that much or almost all of what we call news is not really that, not in the sense of news as a spontaneous happening. Most of "news" is contrived, planted, managed, manipulated, but it is still "news" in that the men reporting it are not managed, manipulated or themselves contriving. WILLIAM SMALL, CBS NEWS

Controversy makes news. We don't cause the controversy; we just report it. We can't ignore it, or assume that if we keep silent the controversy will go away. It's there, it affects a lot of people and we have to report it.

RICHARD GRAF

News was once described as "literature in a hurry." News is a response to <u>now</u>.

The reporter who prepares the immediate hard news story has to respond to events in process. An historian may eventually report the event in perspective, but for now the news reporter has to capture the event as it moves in time.

Reporters are not prophets. They are not omniscient. They do not know the ultimate truth or significance of the events they report. They too are in process. The reporters who heard Lincoln's Gettysburg Address hesitated to spend the telegraph charges to file their stories; the speech seemed so insignificant to most of them. Yet thousands of front-page stories were filed about Clifford Irving's "autobiography" of Howard Hughes, perhaps the best-reported hoax of the century.

All a reporter can do is to bring himself and his resources to the news events of his own lifetime. What we want to examine in this Probe is the unique demand made upon the reporter to screen the moment-by-moment events of today for the massive news audiences who want and need that information.

Veteran broadcast reporter Carole Simpson covered the Chicago Conspiracy Trial for WBBM, CBS radio in Chicago. Your News Input Tape contains recordings of her live radio reports from the Federal Building in Chicago. A transcription of one of these reports follows here. After the news account, Ms. Simpson describes her assignment and the challenge of on-the-spot reporting.

WBBM NEWSRADIO 78
That says it all!

Announcer:

Good afternoon, everyone. The verdicts are in in the Chicago Conspiracy trial. NEWS-RADIO 78 special correspondent, Carole Simpson, has the story.

Carole Simpson:

A split verdict returned in the trial of the Chicago Seven. A ten-woman, two-man jury acquitted two of the conspiracy defendants and found the remaining five guilty of crossing state lines to incite riot. All seven were found "not guilty" of conspiracy and, oddly enough, that's what they called themselves, "The Conspiracy."

Facing a maximum penalty of five years in prison for violations of the new federal anti-riot law, which makes it a crime to cross state lines with the intention of inciting a riot, are 54-year-old David Dellinger, 30-year-old Rennie Davis, 30-year-old Tom Hayden, 33-year-old Abbie Hoffman, and 31-year-old Jerry Rubin. Acquitted of charges they demonstrated and taught the use of incendiary devices were 31-year-old sociologist Lee Weiner and 33-year-old chemistry professor John Froines. Froines broke into tears upon hearing the verdict and it appeared the other defendants were not disappointed by the outcome of their trial.

After the jury was discharged, defense attorney William Kunstler moved immediately for bail, pending an appeal of the convictions, but Judge Hoffman said, "From the evidence and conduct of these defendants on trial, I find they are dangerous men to be at large." He denied bail.

From the Federal Building, this is Carole Simpson reporting for WBBM NEWS-RADIO 78.

Many news stories have come and gone since I covered the Chicago Conspiracy Trial (1969-1970); but I can honestly say it was the most outstanding and nonforgettable story of my reporting career. It was all the more memorable because I was expecting my first child.

After you cover one story for five months, it truly becomes a part of your life. I could scarcely go anywhere after court hours without coworkers, friends, and even strangers asking me: "What's really going on in that courtroom?" Everybody took sides. You were either pro-government and pro-Judge Julius Hoffman (who were seen as defenders of law and order and enforcers of justice) or you were pro-defendants (who were looked upon as victims of political persecution and champions of the oppressed). The trial was only rivaled by the 1968 Democratic Convention as one of the most talked about and controversial stories in recent Chicago history.

I was well prepared to cover the Conspiracy Trial because I had also covered many of the events and disturbances surrounding the Democratic Convention. Before the delegates came to town, I attended news conferences in which some of the defendants announced their plans for massive demonstrations against the war in Viet Nam. I did stories about the self-defense training in anticipation of problems with the police. I heard the threats of putting LSD in the city's drinking water, the plan to nominate a pig for president.

I attended other news conferences in which city officials announced they would not grant parade permits or allow young antiwar activists to camp out in Lincoln Park. I was at O'Hare Field when huge army transport planes unloaded 7,000 federal troops, tanks, trucks, and jeeps for possible riot duty. I was on the convention floor at the Amphitheatre. I was among those tear gassed in Grant Park. The morning after the so-called "Battle of Michigan Avenue," I interviewed demonstrators, their heads swathed in bloody bandages, about their clash with police. After the convention, I heard the charges and countercharges from public officials and sympathizers of every stripe. "It was the demonstrators' fault." "It was the police department's fault."

The U. S. Justice Department indicted 16 people in connection with the convention disturbances: 8 Chicago policemen were charged with violating the civil rights of several persons who were injured, and 8 antiwar activists, including several nationally known radicals, were charged with conspiracy and crossing state lines to incite riots. The 8 policemen were all acquitted.

The trial of the Chicago 7 (originally "8," but Black Panther leader Bobby Seale was severed from the case after his numerous courtroom outbursts) was seen by many as a trial of dissent in America, a trial of the free speech protections of the U. S. Constitution. The defendants represented not only the antiwar movement, but the youth culture, college activism, and the black power movement. Some called it "the trial of the century."

When I was informed I would be assigned to cover the trial, I knew I would witness firsthand an event that would go down in legal history. Approximately 50 to 60 reporters received press credentials--they represented all the major newspapers, wire services, news magazines, radio and television networks.

My job as a radio reporter was considerably different from those of my colleagues in the other news media. The newspaper reporters usually had one story to write and one deadline to meet. The television reporters had two stories to do, one for the early evening newscast, another for the late night report. Reporters for the news magazines had to file one story a week. But I, working for an all-news station, had a deadline at least every hour, sometimes every few minutes when things really broke. I would usually do 10 to 15 reports a day, each from one to two minutes in length. With a phone call into the on-the-air studio, I could go on live almost immediately with details. Radio is the "instant" medium.

When the jury returned the verdicts, we were all locked in the courtroom and were told no one would be allowed to leave until court was adjourned for the day. I was nearly 8 months pregnant and had positioned myself right next to the door because I didn't want to get in the way of what was sure to be a mad dash for the telephones once court was recessed. I wrote my story and awaited my chance. Then one of the marshals opened the door and went out; I sneaked right behind him, made it to the phone, and with a flick of a switch was heard in five cities. I later learned other reporters tried to follow me, but were held back. I was the only one to get out and scooped the nation by about 10 minutes. It became somewhat of a cause celebre, because the national correspondents had been beaten by a black, pregnant woman.

Of course the courtroom was off limits for tape recorders, television and still cameras. So my responsibility as a radio reporter was to be the eyes and ears for the public and to convey with my voice an accurate account of what was happening.

I must admit it was extremely difficult to be objective about the story. I was a reporter, yes, but I was also a human being and an American citizen. I had to struggle to keep my personal opinions out of my reports, to present unbiased accounts of the often frightening and emotion-packed events. (I can't begin to explain what it was like to be in a courtroom under bomb threat, with 25 armed federal marshals lining the walls, with spectator seats jammed with uptight hippies, yippies, and Black Panthers. What it was like to see Bobby Seale chained to a chair and with a gag so big over his mouth, it encircled his head leaving only his eyes and nose visible. What it was like to hear his mumbles through the gag that he wanted to defend himself, that he was being denied his constitutional rights.)

As I said I tried to tell it straight in my news reports. But on several occasions, my news director allowed me to come into the studio and talk with the anchormen about my impressions and feelings. This was clearly identified as personal comment rather than news reporting.

I was never criticized by anyone for being biased in my reports. Both sides thought I was fair. I hope and trust I was.

Did you feel like an eyewitness to history as you listened to the taped news reports or read the transcript?

Carole Simpson acts as a screen between you and the events which took place. She selects and reports. Would you say she was perceptive? Was her language direct and concrete?

Do you think Carole Simpson succeeded in being objective, keeping her own opinions out of the reports?

 YOU ARE THERE

Every member of the class should get a copy of the same newspaper (same date, same edition) and do the following exercise on the news columns.

1 Circle the articles or portions of articles that you think will make their way into history books. Use one color of marking pen for signed articles, another color for unsigned articles.

2 Check back through the circled articles and underline any words or passages that seem slanted or opinionated.

3 Finally label the circled stories to indicate the reporter's vantage on the news. For example, "witness" if he was on the spot and witnessed the event; "interview" if he interviewed witnesses; "recorder" if he worked from documents or announcements; "unknown" if there are no clues to the writer's vantage. Some stories may be combinations of these.

Compare your judgments with those of others in the class. Do you agree on what news events are historic?

Among the "historic" stories, are there more signed articles than unsigned articles?

124

Stories by experienced reporters usually carry a by-line, the reporter's name. Editors also use the by-line to reward outstanding work by less experienced reporters. Judging from the articles you circled, does it appear that the more momentous "historic" stories are handled by more experienced reporters?

Critique and compare the words or passages underlined as slanted. Were any of these found in unsigned articles? In other words, did you have to deal with the opinions of an unknown person?

INTERFACE

Do you ever think you will be included in a history book? Do you think an event you are involved in may be included in a history book?

Do you have any method of sorting out the news items that reach you each day? Is something "important" to you because of its possible impact on history or because of its possible impact on you?

Do you identify with the challenge and excitement of reporting history in the making, or are you indifferent to this?

INVESTIGATE

1 Newswriting as a profession is relatively new. COMPARE the writing of professionally trained newsmen today with the "learning by doing" reporting of the last century. Compare Vietnam and Civil War reporting. Compare the assassination reports of President McKinley and President Kennedy.

2 No national archives keep videotape records of daily TV network newscasts. What effect will this have on future historical research?

There is no question that a reporter can and will interpret facts in his news account. Simply choosing to use one word rather than another, to use one fact and not another is a form of interpretation. No matter how much a newsman tries to "stick to the facts," the best he can do is supply these facts as he knows them. Perfect objectivity is an ideal which the "straight" news reporter aims at, fully aware of his limitations in achieving it.

But some modern newsmen take a different approach. They point out that one distinctive service a newsman can perform is to interpret the facts for his readers. He will be as much concerned with "why" an event happened as he will be with the "who, what, when, and where" of the happening. These newsmen see their professional competence as an ability to interpret and analyze current events. Interpretative reporting, because it gives one man's understanding of the events, always carries a by-line.

The objection raised about interpretative reporting is that a newsman cannot interpret the news without editorializing in the process. His news account may turn out to be a forceful piece of persuasion. The labs which follow have two main purposes: 1) to help you distinguish between interpretative and "straight" news reporting, and 2) to consider how interpretative reporting can respond to your need to know.

 **HISTORY—INTERPRETATION**

Part 1

Have the class select a fairly current news event of sufficient importance that you would expect it to be recorded some day in a high school history book. Three-quarters of the class assume the role of history text writers, and each writer composes a short article for inclusion in next year's revised edition of your high school history book.

The writers should keep in mind that this book will be used in all parts of the country and that the writer's aim is to inform, not to cause the students to make judgments one way or another about the event. Remember that textbook review committees usually demand "objectivity," that is, that the books are not slanted in any way.

The history writers submit their articles at the beginning of a class period, several are chosen at random, duplicated, written on the blackboard, or projected on a screen. One member of the class should then play the role of executive editor of the social science division of the textbook company. He reads each of the articles carefully, then calls each of the writers into his office (in front of the class) to discuss the articles. The aim is history-book objectivity. Are the accounts clear? Are significant facts missing? What emphasis is given to what facts? What recommendations will the editor make?

Repeat the editor-author role play for several of the articles submitted. Then duplicate the manuscripts for class analysis.

Judging from these attempts at straight-fact, objective history writing, what observations would you make about the possibility of "unslanted" news copy?

Those in the class who are not history writers will be anthology editors. Their publishing house has decided to publish a reprint collection of interpretative accounts of the same news event as presented by a number of different newsmen. The anthology editors must conduct an all-out search for interpretative accounts of the news events. They should check the Christian Science Monitor, the National Observer, the New York Times' "News of the Week in Review," the Los Angeles Times, U.S. News and World Report, as well as other metropolitan dailies and national weeklies, AP and UPI signed interpretative articles, and if possible, articles from the underground press. All stories selected should carry a by-line, the newsman's name, because it is essential for the readers to know who is interpreting the news.

Radio scripts for interpretative series like "Dimension," "Monitor," or "Emphasis," are available on request from the New York network offices.

Select those interpreted news accounts that offer the widest cross section of interpretation and reprint the selections for the class. After they have been examined carefully, evaluate the different accounts and compare them with the straight-history accounts.

Do the newsmen draw different conclusions from the same facts?

Which newsmen support their interpretations with more facts?

Were some of the interpretative reports contradictory? If so, does this mean that interpretation is making information mean what the newsmen want it to mean?

What qualities give you confidence in an
interpretative news report?

_____ amount of factual support for the interpretation

_____ reputation of the newsman

_____ reputation of the news medium

_____ writing style of the newsman

_____ sincerity of the newsman, his interest in the story

_____ method of analyzing and relating the facts

_____ the quality of the information, facts other newsmen didn't think
to relate to this story

Make a comparative evaluation of the
history-book articles and the interpreted
news accounts.

Do interpretative news reports force
you to think? to challenge their truth-
fulness?

Based on your findings in this lab, what
criteria would you use to judge the quality of an interpretative news account?

Inside the Conspiracy

By Raymond R. Coffey

"I'm busy," quoth the unquenchable Abbie Hoffman, "working on my speech for when the judge says, 'Do you have any last words before sentence is passed?'"

That offhand verdict was delivered in a courthouse corridor when the Conspiracy 7 trial, now in progress before U.S. District Judge Julius J. Hoffman, was in only its ninth day.

And since then defense attorney William M. Kunstler has declared in open court that he expects his clients to be convicted.

Now the trial—first test of the new federal anti-riot law and second round in the enduring battle over the 1968 Democratic National Convention disorders—is in its eighth week.

The government is expected any day now to wind up presentation of its side of the case, a legal halfway point in what has been billed as one of the most important trials of the times.

WHAT MAKES Abbie Hoffman and his fellow defendants so sure they will be judged guilty? What kind of case has the government presented? What has been going on in that heavily guarded courtroom?

First, much of what has taken place has been irrelevant—irrelevant to the charge against the defendants, irrelevant to the legal process and irrelevant, presumably, to the verdict that will be returned.

These irrelevancies include the shackling, gagging and sentencing of Black Panther Bobby Seale for contempt, a tussle over the defendants' attempt to bring a Viet Cong flag into the courtroom, the defendants' eating jellybeans in court, Abbie Hoffman's blowing kisses to the jury and so on.

In fact, much of the commotion and drama that has engaged the public attention has occurred outside the presence of

Insight

the jury and is not any part of the basis on which the case is going to be judged.

SECOND, the government's case in large part has been based on the public statements of the various defendants before and during the Democratic convention.

The case has been relayed to the jury largely through the testimony of undercover police agents and informers of assorted variety.

There have been more than a dozen such witnesses and their testimony generally has been to the effect that Abbie Hoffman or Jerry Rubin or Tom Hayden or Rennie Davis or another of the defendants said and shouted things like:

"Fight the pigs" or "Hold the park" or "Storm the Hilton" or "Arm yourselves" or "We're going to tear up this town" or "Kick the pigs in the shins" or, even, "Kill the pigs."

THE DEFENDANTS — known as the Conspiracy 8 until Seale was sentenced for contempt and removed to be tried separately later—are charged with conspiracy to incite a riot during the convention. And obviously exhortations like those above could, if heeded, lead to riot.

The defendants do not admit they said all these things. But beyond that, the defense suggests that this kind of testimony only proves that what the government has put on trial is the "political rhetoric" of the defendants and their followers.

Thus, says defense attorney Leonard Weinglass, the government is asking the jury to take seriously and literally an emotional rhetoric that, he says, amounts

Here is an interpretative account of the Chicago Conspiracy Trial. Use the criteria you have cited above to evaluate its quality. What differences can you point out between this report and Carole Simpson's report?

really to the same sort of harmless hyperbolic expression as "Kill the umpire."

Most of what the defendants have been accused of saying was said at public assemblages, some of it even on network television, and not in the kind of secrecy ordinarily associated with conspiracy.

Hence, supporters of the defendants suggest, isn't what they said to be taken in the same vein as former Alabama Gov. George Wallace's veiled threat to run over any demonstrator who lay in front of his car?

Or, in the same vein as Vice President Spiro T. Agnew's campaign charge that Hubert Humphrey was "soft on communism?" Or, Dixie Sen. Strom Thurmond's recent charge that even sincere antiwar demonstrators are "part of the international Communist movement?"

Curious contradictions

One other curious aspect of the government's testimony of "rhetoric" is that it is in several instances contradictory. Which part of it is the jury to take most seriously?

Thus, in addition to the inflammatory exhortations cited previously, some of the government witnesses have conceded that defendants Davis, Hayden and David Dellinger also said on several occasions things like:

They intended only a "peaceful protest," they did "not intend to disrupt the convention," they did "not want violence," and any violence would "come from the police."

The government contends the conspiracy to provoke violence began as early as April, 1968. One of its witnesses, Dwayne Oklepek who infiltrated the demonstration leadership, acknowledged under cross-examination, however, that he had told the FBI that as late as Aug. 21, just before the convention opened, he remained convinced that:

"The desires and efforts of the National Mobilization Committee leaders to have a peaceful demonstration were sincere."

'Prosecutor's dream'

There has been a more damaging kind of testimony than the public rhetoric. This includes testimony about defendant John Froines allegedly masterminding a plot to sow stinkbombs about the Loop, about Froines and defendant Lee Weiner planning to fire bomb the Grant Park underground garage and about small meetings in which plans were laid to disrupt the Loop.

What perturbs the defense more perhaps than any of the testimony is the government's whole approach in trying the defendants for conspiracy—a charge lawyers sometimes refer to as a prosecutor's dream.

It is not necessary in a conspiracy case to prove that any of the illegal actions planned or urged by the defendants actually took place.

NEITHER IS IT necessary to prove that all the defendants met together, secretly or otherwise, and hatched some master plan. In fact, some of the defendants here had never met each other until after the conspiracy indictment was returned last spring.

All the government has to prove under the 1968 anti-riot law is that the defendants used the facilities of interstate commerce or crossed state lines with the "intent" to incite or organize or take part in a riot.

Thus, in effect, the jury is asked to judge the defendants' state of mind. And there is danger of repression in this, the defense contends, particularly in the kind of political climate created by events like the convention disorders and other recent racial and campus disturbances. . . .

INTERFACE

Do you sometimes feel the need for someone to help you interpret an experience that you have had? Do you find a suitable person? What kind of talent do you look for in such a person? perceptiveness? wisdom? maturity? intelligence? sensitivity?

Do your classes ordinarily help you make sense out of information, or do they mainly offer more information input? What is more helpful and satisfying? Do you resent interpretation in the classroom?

Do your school news media do any interpretative reporting? If so, are the interpretations of student reporters respected?

INVESTIGATE

1   Go through back issues of your nearest metropolitan daily paper and make a list of local staff writers who write interpretative news accounts. INTERVIEW several of them separately to find out how they understand news interpretation.

2   ANALYZE one television network's newscasts. How much interpretative reporting is there? Who does the interpreting? What is the normal time-lapse between a news event and the interpretation of it?

3   Interpretation often involves comparing a remote news event with an experience that is close to the local news audience. For instance, NBC's "First Tuesday" report entitled "Orange and Green" interpreted the conflict in Northern Ireland in light of the racial problems in the U.S. EVALUATE your local newsmen's ability to interpret national and international stories in light of local events.

John Linstead, staff writer for the Chicago Daily News, covered the Attica State Prison story in September 1971. The prisoners take-over at Attica was a dramatic piece of "made news." Linstead explains some of the problems a reporter encounters when he deals with "made news."

Many times in covering news events, the reporter finds that the "event" has been created by persons or groups who want to use the newspaper, radio or television to get their message across to the public.

This is often called "made news." It didn't just happen, somebody planned it to illustrate a problem in society or to speak out on an issue.

A press conference is "made news," so is a demonstration. So, in a sense, was the prison riot at the New York State Correctional Facility in Attica, N.Y.

I was sent by my newspaper to cover that story, and shared with perhaps 100 other newsmen some of the worst difficulties in reporting an event many of us had ever had.

And that is unusual with this type of story. Ordinarily with "made news" getting the story is easy, because someone wants to give it to you. The hard part usually comes later, in checking the facts for accuracy, and getting the other side of the story.

But at Attica, one side--the prisoners--wanted to tell its story to reporters, and the other side--the prison administration--did not want that story told. And the administration had all the tools and means--guards, walls, guns-- to keep reporters out that it had to keep prisoners in.

We found out about all that when we gathered in front of the prison--a walled fortress in a bare field on the outskirts of the little farming town of Attica.

We soon discovered that almost our only contact with what was going on inside--where more than 1,000 prisoners held 38 guards hostage--was the public relations man for the state correctional system, Gerald Houlihan.

Now public relations men are hired to tell their bosses' side of the story, and Gerry was no exception. We'd stand outside the prison walls and wait for him to come out--and more often than not, he couldn't answer all our questions. Either he didn't have the information, or he didn't want to tell us the truth.

Finally, the prisoners insisted that television and radio crews and newspaper reporters be allowed in to watch the negotiations with prison authorities. The authorities had to give in, for fear the prisoners would kill the guards.

So we chose "pools," because the administration said there were too many of us to go inside at one time. All the newspaper reporters would elect, or choose by lot, one reporter to go in and report to all of us what went on inside. Television and radio crews did the same, and so did still photographers.

This isn't an ideal arrangement, but it's better than no one seeing what's happening.

But when, after four days, the prison administration decided to attack the prisoners, no reporter was allowed to watch. And that's when the big blunder happened.

When the attack was over, more than 40 persons were dead--nine of them hostages. The prison authorities, the guards, the hostages who lived, all told us that the nine hostages had been killed by the prisoners--that their throats had been cut when the attack began.

And that's the way every one of us wrote the story--and in tremendous detail. Only it wasn't true.

We found that out the next day, when a medical examiner in nearby Monroe County announced the result of his autopsies: All nine hostages had died of gunshot wounds. None of them had been stabbed, slashed or mutilated.

Since the prison administration insisted the prisoners had no guns, that meant the hostages had died from police bullets in the confusion of the attack.

We were angry. We were sure we'd been lied to. The head of the state correctional system, Russell G. Oswald, told us it was all a mistake--that the administration had gotten its information from excited guards and policemen who weren't qualified to tell what happened.

Maybe that was true, maybe not. As often happens, there was no real way to find out the whole truth, no matter how hard we tried.

But one thing all of us newsmen agreed on. The chances of the truth being told the first time would have been a lot greater if newsmen and other outside observers had been able to watch that attack.

The prisoners had a story to tell. If you read the list of demands which Oswald agreed to, you can see that conditions in the prison were very bad. There were beatings, bad food, little exercise, racist attacks.

Since no one would listen to the prisoners' side of the story, they took the drastic step of rioting and taking hostages to make sure the whole country would listen. They created an event.

But though the event was created, the news behind the event--that the prisoners in Attica (and by implication many other prisons) are very badly treated--was real, a legitimate news story.

I often wonder how much different things might have been, how many people would be alive today, if the prisoners had been allowed to tell their story before they felt forced to take drastic action.

Prison rebels ask 'human' treatment

By John Linstead

ATTICA, N.Y.—As a group of reporters on a tour of Attica State Prison passed through prisoner-held Cellblock D, an inmate tapped one newsman on the shoulder and whispered in his ear:

"We're gonna get clobbered when this is all over. We know it. But we want to be treated like human beings."

All the demands, made and reiterated during the three-day siege, all the attempts at negotiation as 1,280 inmates of this maximum security prison watched over their 38 hostages, boiled down to that one whispered request.

AND AMID ALL the hatred festering in the western New York prison the message was getting through.

The prisoners, described by observers as well organized and disciplined, seemed determined not to treat the guards they hold as they say the guards have treated them.

Doctors, clergymen and others who have seen the hostages as they camp out in the Cellblock D courtyard, attest to the humane treatment.

The rebel inmates, after the first few minutes of anger that saw 12 guards injured, some seriously, are reportedly feeding and clothing the hostages, giving them blankets and mattresses and building fires to keep them warm at night and erecting bedsheet tents to ward off the hot midday sun.

A REPORTER who referred to "hostages" was corrected by a prisoner, who said, "They aren't hostages, they're human beings."

Michael Smith, 22, a guard at Attica since February and one of those held hostage, said over television that the "inmates"—then he stopped and corrected himself—the "human beings" were treating him well.

Outside the prison, Michael's father, Stephen, 45, who came from his home in Arcade, 25 miles away, to wait for his son's release said he was proud of what his son had said.

Michael had seemed preoccupied lately, he said, and sometimes complained of the way his fellow guards treated the prisoners. He was optimistic that his son would be safe.

DOWNTOWN on the quiet Main St. of Attica, a few men slumped over the dimly lit bar of the Attica Hotel.

George (no one in the bar would let his last name be printed) mused about prison life and said:

"I've listened to some of these guards talk about the way they treat prisoners and I've known there was trouble brewing up there for a long time."

That brought a response from a white-haired prison guard, Jack, at the other end of the bar. He criticized the public for not supporting prison guards and said the convicts were "beatin' and cuttin'" on the hostages, not letting the 38 receive proper medical aid.

"I don't know how we're gonna get back at 'em," said Jack. "It seems like the administration won't let us. But we're gonna find a way."

AT THE PRISON, the rebellious inmates met with a hastily composed citizens' group trying to reopen negotiations aimed at freeing the hostages.

Among members of the 26-man committee were William M. Kunstler, the attorney; Tom Wicker, associate editor and columnist for the New York Times, and U.S. Rep. Herman Badill (D-N.Y.) and state Sen. Robert Garcia, both Puerto Ricans.

A major sticking point in the negotiations was expected to be the inmates' demand for total amnesty including the pressing of no criminal charges.

The citizens group, which the inmates requested, was pressed into service after direct talks between leaders of the revolt and state authorities broke down.

The inmates have issued several lists of demands ranging from prison reform to asylum in a "non-imperialistic country."

A group of newsmen was allowed to accompany the committee on a tour of Cellblock D and the prison yard, where most of the rebels spent the night.

When a newsman asked an inmate his name, he replied:

"My name is Attica. I am all of us."

Chicago Daily News
September 11, 1971

Does it seem to you that John Linstead remains objective in his report, keeping his personal opinion on the prison controversy out of his story? Or is he biased in some way? Cite examples for your opinion.

FOCUS

Do you believe that the news media have a
responsibility to judge the cause for which
someone is "making" news, or is their
first responsibility to inform the public of
the newsmaking incident?

In retrospect, do you think the newsmaking at Attica had a significant
effect on the nation's awareness of
the prison reform issue?

 "MADE NEWS" AS PUBLIC FORUM

Press conferences, news releases, marches, and demonstrations are all calculated to make news. Public relations men, sales promoters, politicians, and protestors all know the dynamics of "made news" and are constantly trying to make news for themselves, their causes, or their products. As a class monitor the news media for one day looking for "made news" stories. Use weekly periodicals as well. Clip print stories. Describe broadcast stories. Mount each "made news" report on a separate sheet of paper and compile them in a loose leaf binder. Each example should have a blank page facing it in the binder. Then see if you can fill those blank pages with editorials, letters to the editor, notices of speeches and lectures, handbills, or posters that speak out or feed back on the same issue as the "made news" story.

FOCUS)

To what extent could you match "made news" stories with the more traditional use of the media as a public forum?

Which examples seem more effective for bringing an awareness of an issue to the public?

How do you feel about those who "made" news? Do your feelings vary according to the issue? the method of newsmaking? the people who "made" the news?

 **NEWSMAKERS**

People make news. And certain people are automatic newsmakers. They provide ready-made news. Sometimes it is because of what they are doing or what they are saying. Sometimes it is because of the prominence or fascination of their personalities. A celebrity, a crusader, an elected government official can make news simply because of who he is. People are interested in him, and therefore in what he does, what he says, and what happens to him.

Get copies of today's newspaper and current issues of weekly news magazines. List below all the prominent newsmakers you can find. Where a person makes news simply because of his or her personality and not because of the importance of his words or action, place a check after his name.

Newsmakers:

Judging from the data you have gathered, what conclusions can you draw about how news media use newsmakers to attract or maintain audiences?

Do the most obvious newsmakers in your school show an understanding of the schedules, deadlines, and audiences of the school news media? of the local community media? Do they tend to bring news to the attention of the newsmen, or do they have to be sought out by newsmen?

The story behind the story provides another type of news, frequently important news that affects our decision making. This is not the news that happens or is "staged." It is the news that originates when an alert reporter like William Jones picks up a lead, a hunch, a suspicion, and begins digging for a story. Investigative reporting is often most effective when it is used to reveal corruption in business and politics, to protect the oppressed, the little people, the powerless citizens. Serving this important "watchdog" function in society has earned journalists the title of the Fourth Estate.

The story which follows was the first in a six-part series for which William Jones won the 1971 Pulitzer Prize for local reporting.

Men of mercy? Profit in pain

By William Jones

They are the misery merchants and they prowl the streets of our city 24 hours a day as profiteers of human suffering.

Waiting in filthy garages scattered thruout the city, they prey on families faced with an urgent need for transportation and medical care for a loved one.

They are the hustlers among the city's private ambulance operators and they are waiting for your call for help.

Their business is big business in Chicago. The multimillion-dollar industry accounts for nearly 1 million dollars of Cook county's welfare fees each year.

At the same time, the misery merchants are exacting a toll in needless suffering and sadistic treatment of the ill that may never be inventoried.

Play Russian Roulette

You may have to call the misery merchants this afternoon or tomorrow or next week. When you do, a member of your family may be gasping after a heart attack or screaming in agony after fracturing a hip or leg. As you frantically leaf thru the telephone directory to find an ambulance company, you unwittingly will be playing a game of Russian roulette with the person you are trying to help.

The stakes are high. If you are poor or black or on welfare, they are even higher. I know because I

worked as a misery merchant and this is how they operate:

1. A middle-age man lies gasping from an apparent heart attack in his north side apartment. His throat makes a rasping sound as he desperately tries to continue breathing. A two-man ambulance crew stands over his body, arguing with a friend of the victim that the $40 fee must be paid before the man is placed on the stretcher. They are told the victim has only two dollars in cash. The crew shrugs, then lifts the still gasping man onto a kitchen chair where he slumps across the table. As they walk out of the apartment one of the attendants reaches across the table and pockets the two dollars.

A Plea Ignored

2. An elderly black man, his body wracked with cancer, pleads with a private ambulance crew to handle him gently because even the slightest pressure causes extreme pain. The attendant in charge ignores his plea and grabs the man under the arms, drags him across the floor to the stretcher, and drops the patient. As the old man's face contorts in agony and breaks into a sweat, the attendant mutters to his fellow worker: "Next time the guy will walk to the stretcher."

3. An epileptic with a fractured hip lies in the rear of a police squadrol for nearly two hours until a private ambulance firm that makes payoffs to policemen is able to respond to the call. Instead of taking the victim to a hospital in the squadrol, the police spend a dime to call a misery merchant. Then they wait until the ambulance—and the $10 payoff—arrive. When the ambulance finally responds, the victim is ordered to crawl from the squadrol onto the stretcher. Hospital records later will be falsified to show that the victim was picked up at a neighbor's home.

"She Looks All Right"

4. An ambulance crew demands that a northwest side housewife with a broken back write out a $49 check as she lies in a hospital. When she complains that the pain is making it difficult for her to perform the task, they fill out the check and hand it back to her to sign.

5. An ambulance driver hurls insults at a black woman while her daughter waits for emergency transportation after suffering a miscarriage. The daughter is screaming. "She looks all right," the ambulance driver decides. "She can walk down the stairs." The apartment is on the third floor. It is raining and once outside the victim is ordered to crawl into the ambulance thru a side door.

These are a few of the incidents observed during a two-month investigation of the misery merchants by THE TRIBUNE and the Better Government association. The probe was prompted by complaints from other ambulance operators who told of payoffs to police and firemen, welfare fraud, and sadistic treatment of the ill and injured. . . .

Chicago Tribune
June 7, 1970

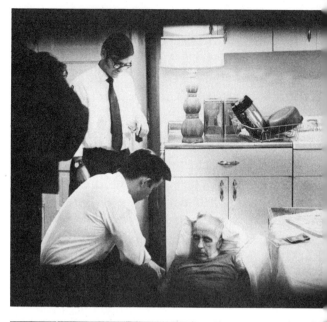

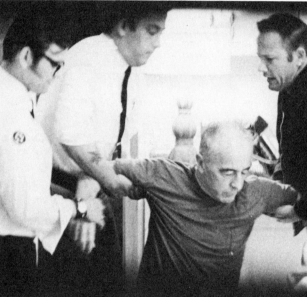

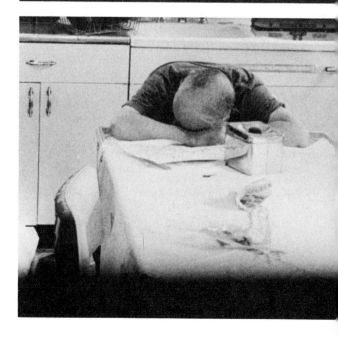

140

We called them the "misery merchants." They were the operators of some of Chicago's largest private ambulance companies and for two months I lived and worked with them.

The result was a six-part series that exposed sadistic mistreatment of the ill and injured, police bribes and welfare fraud. A grand jury indicted 16, including 10 policemen, on charges ranging from bribery to theft.

There is a great feeling of satisfaction in uncovering and publishing such a scandal. In this case, The Tribune used its resources to act for thousands of poor citizens. These people had no way to cry out against watching a loved one carelessly handled and even berated for daring to need emergency medical transportation.

As I watched it happen, I found myself feeling the same sense of rage and helplessness. This was one of the pitfalls of the investigation, the mental depression that comes after days of watching such abuses. I frequently found myself eager to end the undercover venture as quickly as possible in order to expose and perhaps put an end to the abuses.

But at the same time, I realized that, by breaking the story prematurely, I could very well be ignoring the same kinds of activities among the ambulance crews. For this reason, William Recktenwald, a Better Government Association investigator who also worked as an attendant, and I forced ourselves to work for as many firms as possible.

We also found that threats and personal risks are always a part of undercover work. At one point, the vice president of one large ambulance firm became suspicious. He warned me during a late-night confrontation that a beating awaited me if I were a private investigator. I managed to talk my way through the interrogation with a few well chosen jokes about James Bond spies.

About a week after the series was published and official action was beginning to mount, a tipster warned me of a meeting that allegedly took place at one of the ambulance firms. He said there were guns and money on the desk and that a company official had told his crew members "$5,000 goes to the guy who blows off Jones' or Recktenwald's head."

I considered the warning serious enough to move my family out of our home for several days and sought the additional security of an armed bodyguard.

As the series unfolded, many agencies took swift action. In addition to grand jury indictments, the city council passed tough, new laws controling ambulance companies and the training of attendants. The fire department added a new fleet of ambulances and changed its policies to provide better service to citizens.

Now these corrective measures are in effect, the threats and depression have gradually faded. Instead I have the personal satisfaction of having taken part in something that has really changed things for the better for others.

In investigative reporting, those who are
exposed for their wrongdoing will normally
deny the truth of the report. What characteristics can you look for in the report
that will give you reason to believe it? Do
you find these in Bill Jones' report?

A reader is easily stirred to anger against
those who harm the little people. Do you
think Jones takes advantage of this fact,
or does he keep his report detached enough
so as not to incite mob action?

How would you compare an investigative
reporter to a police investigator? Do you
think Jones would function well on the
police force?

INVESTIGATION SURVEY

Identify instances of investigative reporting in the different media. Reflect on your
recent experience and cite instances where the media has reported in-depth stories
of significant human, social, or political concern.

Newspapers

Magazines

Radio

Television

LAB THE COST OF INVESTIGATING

Investigative reporting demands time. It often requires a team of reporters. Both of these elements call for considerable financial investment, and so news media with small budgets find this kind of reporting difficult, sometimes impossible. Investigative reporting is more commonly found in those media with a broad financial base, such as network news, large urban dailies, and national news periodicals. For example, Wall Street Journal, Time, Newsweek, the Christian Science Monitor.

Compare your own daily newspaper with the Wall Street Journal, or the New York Times, or the Christian Science Monitor. Your local library will probably have all these papers.

> You will find no real muckraking by the richest man in town.   EDWARD R. MURROW

FOCUS

Has your local daily published any investigative reports carried out by members of its own news staff?

What about the national dailies?

What areas of public concern were covered in these investigations?

Can you cite situations, agencies, publically funded projects, or specialized activity in your community that might be the subject of an investigative report by local newsmen?

In its effort to bring about reform, which is the more powerful weapon of the news media, the investigative report or the editorial?

INTERFACE

Have you ever had to struggle with a topic for independent study
that required a lot of time, patience, persistence, and ingenuity;
and yet there was always the possibility that the search would come
to nothing? If so, how did you feel about the experience? Why did
you persist in the investigation?

Have any students in your school ever produced a true investigative
exposé and reported it through school-sponsored or alternative
media?

Suppose that a student reporter decided to do an exposé in your
school on bogus assignments and term papers, homework that is
not the work of the person handing it in. Suppose he struck up
several friendly conversations with you and your friends about your
own assignment work. How would you feel about the reporter's
methods when the story broke? Can you approve of the undercover
tactics for the good of the exposé? even if the tactics are used on
you?

INVESTIGATE

INVESTIGATE the era of the muckrakers in United States history. How did Lincoln
Steffins affect city politics? How did Ida Tarbell affect the great monopolies like
the railroads and Standard Oil?

DRAW UP a list of media titles and reporters whose main claim to fame has been
their consistent ability to expose through investigative reporting.

"Name of the Game" based its plot lines on the excitement and danger of investigative reporting. INTERVIEW a good investigative reporter on his reaction to the
TV series.

Observation or Involvement: what's the difference?

PROBE

The newest breed of reporter goes beyond observation into the realm of involvement. These reporters engage in live-ins with their notebooks, tape recorders, and cameras. Gay Talese's Honor Thy Father and Tom Wolfe's Kandy-Kolored Tangerine-Flake Streamline Baby are prominent examples of this style of reporting, a style encouraged by Esquire magazine in the early 1960's.

Sometimes living-in is the only adequate way to report a newsworthy situation. There was no other way John Howard Griffin could have written Black Like Me. A newsman may choose to become personally involved in the news situation if he decides that it is important for his readers to experience the feelings, the emotions, and the personal relationships that are rarely revealed in a more detached style of reporting. Three months of living in will normally sensitize a writer in a way that will dramatically affect his finished report.

This involvement style of reporting is commonly referred to as the New Journalism. The lab which follows is set up to help you discover the difference between observation and involvement reporting.

LAB LIVE-IN REPORTING

Have you ever read a reporter's version of what your school is like, a report in a local newspaper or perhaps even in an area or national publication? The reporter probably had little more than a day to gather facts for the assignment.

The following pages contain two news stories on the same school. The first was put together as a straight news story, the other was written after a three-month live-in.

Malcolm X College's new look

By Betty Washington

The new Malcolm X City College was christened in blackness Tuesday by students who promised to use the school both as a learning center and as a liberating force in the black community.

Students and faculty members marched the two blocks from the old Nat Turner Branch of the campus, 1757 W. Harrison, to the new $26 million building at 1900 W. Van Buren.

Once inside the new school's red-carpeted auditorium, the 2,000 students and faculty members stood with clenched fists upraised and sang the black national anthem, "Lift Every Voice and Sing."

CHARLES G. Hurst Jr., president of Malcolm X, told the audience that the dedication ceremony was the "beginning of the process to liberate our community."

Hurst also listed dignity and love as well as black excellence as "virtues of the African people."

Then the voice was replaced by the sound of African drums and young men and women filled the circular stage with rhythmic definitions of their roles as community college students and as participants in the spirit of Pan-Africanism.

Detmar D. Timberlake, student government president, looked around the three-story building that replaced two overcrowded Malcolm X campuses on the West Side, and summed up his feelings about the new school:

"We are a true community college," he said. "It's a good feeling, brothers."

Chicago Daily News
April 14, 1971

'I Was a White Student at Malcolm X'

What is it like to be virtually the only white man among black people who feel that they and their ancestors have been systematically victimized for generations by whites? Fredric Soll got a clear answer shortly after he began attending Malcolm X College this semester without disclosing his identity as a TRIBUNE reporter. This is the first of his reports.

BY FREDRIC SOLL

I'm the man. Whitey. I went down under in the black nub of Chicago.

It is black man's land. Black bleeds from the walls, the pavement; it flies from the flagpole. Most everything else has been cultured out. Black is the look, the touch, the sound of the talk.

But that's the plan.

Clenched, Black Fist

The school trademark at Malcolm X Community College is a clenched, black fist and the school hero and namesake—Malcolm X—used to say that black folks have it bad because a seething, invulnerable racism burns inside the collective white soul.

The students believe it. Every fiber in the body of nearly every student here seems to believe it—to know it. The fabric of their individual lives has proved it, nourished it. The "blackness" just gives the belief form, sculpting words out of boulders of frustration.

At Malcolm X, 1900 W. Van Buren St., I never forgot the color of my skin. I'm the contrast. The ferocity of black assertion burned the whiteness deep into my consciousness.

Forced to Justify Whiteness

Since the day I registered as a freshman at the beginning of the spring semester, I was forced to justify my whiteness to a black world which is accepting no excuses. Blacks say they have heard all they want to hear about the accidents of heredity.

While standing in line on registration day and waiting for a guidance counselor to approve my schedule, I watched the students ahead of me get encouragement and smiles and "right-ons." I got icy stares that invited me to drop out before I began.

I cleared out tables at the cafeteria whenever I sat down and conversations suddenly stopped while I passed them by.

Tolerated, as Roach Is

I was tolerated at Malcolm X; no more and no less than the cockroaches black people have put up with on the West Side. . . . "The man's gonna be around, you can spray, you can shout, but he'll always be around."

It all happened because of my skin color. There was no other reason.

By the end of the first day I wanted to take the next black face I saw—any face, as long as it was black—and rub it in cement until there was nothing left. They were sticking it to me for nothing I had said or done.

I felt I'm as good as they are, as smart as they are; just as human. It was happening because I'm white; nothing more.

So it turned my stomach, tied me up in knots. Rage. Frustration. Confusion. The rhetoric of racism, until now only a yell from the other side, was becoming a personal reality. I was being nailed because of the color of my skin and the truth of that is devastating. It made me want to strike back, take what they wouldn't give.

Maybe, I was feeling like a black man. It was just a germ's worth, but maybe I was getting an inkling of what it's like to be on the underbelly of a two-colored rainbow, where the pot of gold is completely out of sight.

But it was no more than a germ's worth. There are whole lumps of hate and fear I will never understand. My rage could be siphoned off each night back on the North Side, where white is king. Black people have few such sanctuaries.

"This Is My Place"

"I feel like this is my place," Sandra, a second-year student at Malcolm X, told me. "This is sanctuary for *me*. But what the hell are you doing here? Aren't there enough white schools?"

"Black Pride." "Black Excellence." Words that cover the Malcolm X campus. They are stenciled in the doors, written on the walls, chalked on the boards, tied to the people's tongues. It is a conscious, saturation display. There has been a grab for anything

that is distinctly black as if the deluge of color-consciousness and color-pride will somehow obliterate generations of boot-black mentality.

African art fills the school with careful design: Anything that smacks of the man just isn't there.

The school is spotless; it glitters.

"Ain't Gonna Hassle Us"

"Look man," one student told me. "If you mess up your place, you're just a sloppy white man. If I mess *this* place up, I'm a nigger. If I throw my cigaret butts on the floor, I'm doing just what the man says we always do when we 'get something nice.' So we're being careful. You ain't gonna be able to hassle us on the small stuff anymore."

Malcolm X students say they are the "new blacks." They are thrice removed from the fathers of the '30s and '40s who bleached their skin and straightened their hair in order to water down the curse of their color; twice removed from the passive resistant civil rights Negro; and once removed from the burn-it-down nigger who erupted after Martin Luther King's death.

The people at Malcolm X have turned inward; they have time only to be interested in their own; their own people, community, school, and individual destinies.

Don't Like His Ways

"Hate serves no useful function; it just wastes my time," said Brother Hood, 22, a second-year student. "I don't hate the white man. I just don't like his ways."

Malcolm X people are not after whitey. They just ignore him when he's around. There's really no reason to fear—the students are far more interested in not messing up themselves and their school than in messing up the man.

But after a while, I began to wish they would hate me—anything other than the kind of well-adjusted tolerance that made me feel like a disease. The black man has learned well from the white. He can elicit rage by doing absolutely nothing.

Chicago Tribune
March 26, 1972

FOCUS

Does the involvement style of newswriting
draw you into the news event more so than
the straight news story? If so, what values
do you see in this type of news reporting?

Does this involvement style of writing cloud
your ability to judge the accuracy and reliability of the story?

Is a school report a good subject for this
type of involvement reporting? What other
subjects would be suitable?

INTERFACE

Have you ever been involved in a situation or event which was reported in the news? How did you feel about the adequacy of the
report? Was it accurate? Was it complete enough? Would it have
been different if the reporter had been involved in the event?

How would you have reported the event you cited above?

Is there a cause, an activity, or a program you are sufficiently
involved in that your local or school news media might assign you
to do an in-depth story on it?

INVESTIGATE

1   PREPARE a bibliography of books and magazine articles on the New Journalism.
Display some of the material so others in the class may read them.

2   Charles Lindbergh was a newsmaker who became a reporter after the fact when
he wrote We. COMPARE his reporting with that of a new journalist who enters into
an experience, for instance sky diving, in order to report it more adequately.

3   INVESTIGATE the emergence of cinema verité. Screen one of the early French
films if possible.

SIMULATE Using the insights and conclusions you arrived at above, role play the following Media Man Simulation.

You are a member of the Washington Press Corps, a reporter for your daily newspaper. A major press conference with the President of the United States has been announced. It will be broadcast tonight over national television. What questions will you prepare to ask the President? Would you want to bring up unexpected issues, test the President's character under stress, and make news that way? In fairness to your readers, will you give them a straight account of the press conference, or will you interpret the event?

Critique of the News

Good news is no news.   EDWARD R. MURROW

There is a well-known truism about news that defines it as something out of the ordinary. It says that if a dog bites a man it is not news, but that if a man bites a dog, it is news.
                                          DUANE BRADLEY

The news as presented in both broadcast and newsprint does tend to give a startling, not a balanced presentation of the day's events, as James Reston has put it. The television camera or the newspaper headline focuses, like a flashlight beam in the darkness, at what has just moved. All else is lost in the limbo.   ERIC SEVAREID

Instead of a whole, balanced view of life, TV news offers a "slice of life" peek, a close-up of the flash-points that are igniting society.   RICHARD TOWNLEY

Once again, if the quality of our lives depends upon what we know and how well we are informed, and the news does make a significant contribution to this, it will be important for us to be aware of those limitations which may seriously affect the quality of the news we receive.

A century ago at least eight New York City daily newspapers battled one another in circulation warfare. The weapons were sensational headlines, newspaper Extras, and news stunts like reporter Stanley's search for Dr. Livingston in Africa. The newspaper wars undoubtedly weakened the value of competent reporting; everything was judged in terms of its power to sell papers, its immediate reader rewards.

Although total circulation figures continued to rise, the number of daily newspapers steadily declined after 1900. The main threat to the papers was no longer another newspaper's presses down the street but the radio towers rising up all over the place. Radio had speed, and it taught people to expect the latest information break right now. What followed was predictable, on-the-spot reporting, cameras and microphones set up in anticipation of news, and electronic news consumers with tubes and transistors going most of the day.

The lab that follows offers an example of the rush to be immediate, the rush to give the news consumer what he wants now, so that he will tune in the same radio station or the same channel tomorrow, sustaining the ratings and the sponsors.

 BROADCAST WIRE

The following sequence of news bulletins and stories are from the Associated Press broadcast wire service for July 5, 1970. Analyze the reports and note how this unexpected fast-breaking story developed from the first bulletin to the last story.

Note: Your local newspaper or broadcast station may be happy to give you 12 hours of wire copy so you can trace the development of a current unexpected fast-breaking story from first bulletin to final report.

URGENT   9:54 a.m.

PLANE (TOPS)

(TORONTO) --AN AIR CANADA AIRLINER BOUND FROM MONTREAO
TO LOS ANGELES HAS CRASHED NEAR TORONTO INTERNATIONAL
AIRPORT.

FIRST REPORTS SAID THE PLANE CARRIED 97 PERSONS. BUT
THERE IS NO IMMEDIATE WORD ON DEATHS OR INJURIES.

THERE WAS CONFUSION AMONG WITNESSES AS TO WHAT HAPPENED.
ONE SAID THE PLANE EXPLODED IN THE AIR BEFORE CRASHING.
ANOTHER SAID IT PLUNGED TO THE GROUND AND THEN EXPLODED.

ONTARIO PROVINCIAL POLICE SAID THE PLANE CAME DOWN IN
AN AREA 18 MILES NORTHWEST OF DOWNTOWN TORONTO.

POLICE WERE TRYING TO CLEAR TRAFFIC ON HIGHWAYS AROUND
THE AREA TO ALLOW AMBULANCES TO REACH THE SCENE.

IN FIRST LINE OF ABOVE READ CITY X X X MONTREAL.

-NINTH FIVE-MINUTE SUMMARY-   10:04 a.m.

HERE IS THE LATEST NEWS FROM THE ASSOCIATED PRESS-

(TORONTO) - AN AIR CANADA D-C-8 HAS CRASHED ON APPROACH
TO TORONTO INTERNATIONAL AIRPORT. IT WAS ON A FLIGHT FROM
MONTREAL TO LOS ANGELES WITH A SCHEDULED STOP IN TORONTO.
FIRST REPORTS SAID THERE WERE 97 PERSONS ABOARD. THERE HAS
BEEN NO IMMEDIATE WORD ON DEATHS OR INJURIES. SOME
WITNESSES SAID THE PLANE CRASHED AND THEN EXPLODED. OTHERS
SAID IT EXPLODED IN THE AIR BEFORE CRASHING.

(TORONTO) - NINETY-SEVEN PERSONS ARE BELIEVED DEAD IN
THE CRASH OF AN AIR-CANADA D-C-8 JET NEAR TORONTO. THE
PLANE WAS BOUND FROM MONTREAL TO LOS ANGELES WITH A STOP
IN TORONTO.

AN EYEWITNESS SAYS HE SAW AN ENGINE BURNING JUST BEFORE
THE JETLINER CRASHED THIS MORNING. JOSEPH BOTTING SAYS HE
WAS PLAYING GOLF WHEN HE LOOK UP. BOTTING SAYS THE PLANE
STARTED TO CLIMB. . . THEN THE ENGINE FELL OFF. . . THE
PLANE WENT INTO A VERTICAL DIVE. . . AND EXPLODED IN A
HUGE FIREBALL.

THE CRASH SITE IS IN A FARM FIELD, ABOUT FIVE MILES
NORTHWEST OF TORONTO INTERNATIONAL AIRPORT. THE PLANE
WAS IN ITS APPROACH FOR THE STOP IN TORONTO WHEN IT
CRASHED

ONTARIO PROVINCIAL POLICE HAVE CORDONED OFF A TEN
SQUARE MILE AREA AND ARE CLEARING CARS OFF TWO MAJOR
HIGHWAYS TO MAKE WAY FOR EMERGENCY EQUIPMENT.

AIR CANADA SAID THE PLANE WAS DUE TO LAND AT 8:15 A.M.
AND THAT THE CRASH OCCURRED AS THE BIG PLANE WAS IN A
GLIDE PATH ABOUT 8,000 YARDS FROM THE AIRPORT RUNWAY.
A SPOKESMAN SAID AS IT MOVED DOWM AN ENGINE FELL OFF AND
ONE OF THE WINGS COLLAPSED.

AN AIR CANADA OFFICIAL SAID OF THE 97 PERSONS ABOARD,
ONLY 70 WERE PAYING PASSENGERS. THERE WAS A CREW OF NINE
AND THE REST WERE AIR CANADA PERSONNEL TRAVELING TO LOS
ANGELES OR TORONTO.

BULLETIN (AP)   11:34 a.m.

(TORONTO)--AIR CANADA SAYS ALL 106 PERSONS ABOARD
WERE KILLED IN THE CRASH OF AN AIR CANADA JETLINER THIS
MORNING NEAR TORONTO.

IT SAYS THE PLANE CARRIED 97 PASSENGERS AND A CREW OF
NINE.

MORE AP 081   (TORONTO-PLANE) X X X AIRPORT. 11:58 a.m.

THE TOTAL ABOARD WAS REVISED UPWARD TO 106 BY AIR
CANADA AS DETAILS WERE FORWARDED TO ITS TORONTO OFFICE
FROM MONTREAL.

THE DEAD INCLUDED 75 PAYING PASSENGERS, 22 AIR CANADA
EMPLOYEES AND A CREW OF NINE. THAT INCLUDED THREE PILOTS
AND SIX OTHERS.

IT'S THE SECOND WORST AIR CRASH IN CANADA'S HISTORY.
THE WORST ALSO INVOLVED AN AIR CANADA D-C-EIGHT. THAT WAS
A CRASH ON NOVEMBER 29TH, 1963 NEAR STE. THERESE, QUEBEC
IN WHICH ALL 118 ABOARD WERE KILLED.

TODAY'S CRASH INVOLVED A SUPER D-C-EIGHT. IT WAS DUE
TO LAND AT TORONTO AIRPORT AT 8:15 A.M. EDT WHEN IT
CRASHED ABOUT 8,000 YARDS FROM THE RUNWAY.

HERE IS THE LATEST NEWS FROM THE ASSOCIATED PRESS: 1:22 p.m.

(TORONTO)--AIR CANADA OFFICIALS REPORT ALL 106
PASSENGERS ABOARD A JET THAT CRASHED THIS MORNING WERE
KILLED. WHILE THE SUPER DC-8 WAS MAKING A LANDING
APPROACH INTO TORONTO SHORTLY AFTER EIGHT O'CLOCK (EDT)
ONE OF ITS ENGINES CAUGHT FIRE AND FELL OFF A WITNESS
SAYS PIECES FLUTTERED DOWN FROM A WING. THE AIRCRAFT WENT
INTO A VERTICAL DIVE. THERE WAS A HUGE FIREBALL. THE PLANE
CRASHED IN A FARM FIELD ABOUT FOUR MILES FROM THE TORONTO
AIRPORT.

THOSE ABOARD INCLUDED 97 PASSENGERS AND NINE CREW
MEMBERS.

THE DC-8 IN THIS MORNING'S CRASH WAS ON A FLIGHT FROM
MONTREAL TO LOS ANGELES, WITH A SCHEDULED STOP AT TORONTO.
OF THE PASSENGERS ABOARD, 75 HAD PAID FARES; THE 22 OTHERS
WERE AIR CANADA EMPLOYEES.

IT WAS THE SECOND MAJOR FOREIGN AIR DISASTER IN 36
HOURS AND THE SECOND WORST IN CANADA. SEVEN YEARS AGO,

118 PERSONS DIED IN A TRANS CANADA AIRLINES CRASH IN
QUEBEC SEVEN YEARS AGO.

THE WEATHER WAS PERFECT AT THE TIME OF THE ACCIDENT.
AN EYEWITNESS DESCRIBED THE CRASH SCENE IN THESE WORDS:
"IT LOOKED LIKE SOMEONE HAD TURNED OVER A THOUSAND
GARBAGE CANS."

AP118   3:22 p.m.

HERE IS THE LATEST FIVE MINUTE NEWS FROM THE ASSOCIATED PRESS

(TORONTO) AN AIR CANADA D-C-8 HAS PLOWED INTO THE
BACKYARD OF A FARMHOUSE NEAR TORONTO INTERNATIONAL AIRPORT
KILLING ALL 108 (CORRECT) PERSONS ABOARD. MOST OF THE
PASSENGERS WERE AMERICANS RETURNING HOME FROM THE JULY
FOURTH WEEKEND. THE PLANE WAS ON A FLIGHT FROM MONTREAL
TO LOS ANGELES, WITH A SCHEDULED STOP IN TORONTO.

THE PLANE NOSEDIVED SHORTLY AFTER THE PILOT RADIOED
THE AIRPORT THAT ONE OF HIS ENGINES WAS AFIRE. A POLICE
SPOKESMAN SAID THE CONTROL TOWER ORDERED THE PILOT TO
GAIN ALTITUDE AND JETTISON FUEL. AS HE WAS COMPLYING THE
ENGINE FLEW OFF AND FELL ONTO A RUNWAY. SECONDS LATER
ANOTHER PART OF THE PLANE FELL. THE JET HIT THE GROUND
WITH A TREMENDOUS BLAST ONLY 75 FEET FROM A FARMHOUSE.

C O R R E C T I O N   3:22 p.m.

IN THE ABOVE SUMMARY, FIRST ITEM -- PLANE -- READ
THIRD LINE XXX MANY OF THE PASSENGERS WERE AMERICANS
(MANY, INSTED MOST)

AP186R

PLANE CRASH (TOPS)   9:54 p.m.

(TORONTO)--AN "AIR CANADA" JETLINER CARRYING 1o8 PERSONS,
MORE THAN 20 OF THEM AMERICANS, PLOWED INTO THE BACKYARD
OF A FARMHOUSE WHILE APPROACHING TORONTO INTERNATIONAL
AIRPORT TODAY. ALL 108 ABOARD PERISHED.

IT WAS THE SECOND-WORST DISASTER IN CANADA'S HISTORY--
AND THE SECOND PLANE ACCIDENT IN THREE DAYS TO CLAIM MORE
THAN 100 LIVES. A BRITISH JET CRASHED NEAR BARCELONA,
SPAIN ON FRIDAY WITH 112 ABOARD.

THE CANADIAN SUPER D-C-8 WAS ON A FLIGHT FROM MONTREAL
TO LOS ANGELES. IT NOSED-DIVED SHORTLY AFTER THE PILOT

RADIOED THE TORONTO AIRPORT THAT ONE OF HIS ENGINES WAS
ON FIRE.

A POLICE SPOKESMAN SAID THE CONTROL TOWER ORDERED THE
PILOT TO GAIN ALTITUDE AND JETTISON FUEL. WHILE HE WAS
DOING SO, THE ENGINE FLEW OFF THE PLANE AND FELL ON THE
RUNWAY.

AN AIRLINE SPOKESMAN SAID THE PLANE TOUCHED THE RUNWAY
ONCE, "BOUNCED" INTO THE AIR AND THEN THUNDERED TO THE
GROUND ONLY 75 FEET FROM THE FARMHOUSE.

THE FARMER SAID THE "TREMENDOUS BLAST" BLEW OUT THE
BACK DOOR AND WINDOWS OF HIS FRAME HOME.

THE JET HAD ONLY BEEN IN SERVICE FOUR WEEKS. IT HAD
FLOWN 494 HOURS.

IT WAS PILOTED BY CAPTAIN PETER HAMILTON, 49, A 24-
YEAR VETERAN OF AIR CANADA AND A FORMER PRESIDENT OF THE
CANADIAN AIR LINES PILOTS ASSOCIATION.

MICHAEL MATYAS, WHO WAS TAKING HIS SON TO THE AIRPORT,
WITNESSED THE CRASH AND SAID ONE ENGINE BURST INTO FLAME.

HE REPORTED: "THERE WERE FLAMES ON THE BOTTOM REAR OF THE
PLANE, THEN LOTS OF SMOKE...THEN IT JUST NOSE-DIVED RIGHT
DOWN."

1:04 a.am.   July 6

(TORONTO) -- AN AIR CANADA JETLINER CARRYING 108
PERSONS, INCLUDING MORE THAN 20 AMERICANS, CRASHED AT
TORONTO INTERNATIONAL AIRPORT SUNDAY KILLING ALL ABOARD.
THE AIR CANADA SUPER D-C-8, ON A FLIGHT FROM MONTREAL TO
LOS ANGELES, WENT DOWN SECONDS AFTER THE PILOT INFORMED
THE CONTROL TOWER THAT HE HAD MISSED HIS APPROACH AND
WOULD TRY AGAIN.

THE AIRCRAFT APPARENTLY ROLLED FOR A SHORT DISTANCE
ALONG THE RUNWAY AND THEN BEGAN WHAT APPEARED TO BE A
NORMAL TAKEOFF FOR A NEW APPROACH. WHILE STILL ABOVE THE
RUNWAY, THE OUTER RIGHT ENGINE DROPPED OFF AND THE INNER
RIGHT ENGINE FELL AWAY BEFORE THE PLANE HIT THE GROUND.
IT CRASHED IN THE BACKYARD OF A FARMHOUSE.

1   Using the time of each bulletin as an indicator, list the sources for the story as
they evolved.

2 A news story like the one above obviously becomes more accurate and comprehensive as time allows for more information gathering. Early inaccuracies are inevitable, but note how many are actually corrected in succeeding reports when newsmen receive more information from better sources.

3 Noting the kinds of facts included in the first wire accounts of the crash, and noting the sources cited, describe the characteristics of the fast-breaking news story.

<u>Characteristics</u>   <u>Supporting data</u>

The following article on the crash appeared in newspapers on the evening of July 6, about 35 hours after the crash. Notice that the wire service is Reuters, an international service with home offices in England.

Air crash killing 108 probed

TORONTO, Canada (Reuters) — Canadian officials today pieced together information in an attempt to discover what caused the crash of an Air Canada jetliner Sunday that took the lives of 108 persons, 22 of them Americans.

The flight recorder was discovered last night 150 feet from the wreckage of the plane. The box, attached to the rear underside of the aircraft to gather vital information, was reportedly undamaged, and officials hoped to get from it facts on flight conditions and aircraft performance.

The plane crashed into a farm field, only a short distance from a house, after apparently attempting to make a scheduled landing at Toronto's Malton Airport while en route from Montreal to Los Angeles.

The sun was shining and the weather was generally clear when the crash occurred.

There was no report from the pilot of any trouble, an Air Canada official said, until the plane was in its landing approach. The pilot then told the Malton control tower, according to a flight controller there, that one of the DC8's starboard engines was on fire.

The controller said he ordered the pilot to gain altitude and jettison fuel. According to another eyewitness, the pilot did this after touching the runway at one point.

Observers said that when the plane was in the air again the engine fell off. Other parts of the plane also began to drop off. Minutes later the plane plummeted to the ground.

FOCUS

How does the organization and emphasis of this later Reuters report differ from the early AP broadcast wire reports?

What qualities, if any, that you noted as being characteristic of fast-breaking news stories do not apply to the later newspaper wire report?

How many people would have needed the crash information as quickly as the broadcast media got it to them? Example: Drivers in the immediate area of the crash -- blocked highways.

How many fast-breaking stories do you remember that have immediately affected your decisions? Based on the data in this lab, suggest guidelines and precautions for making decisions with fast-breaking information.

INTERFACE

Most people like to be the first to know the news. When you are the first or among the first to know, do you enjoy being able to tell others while it is still an "exclusive" story?

A school has many fast-breaking stories. How are they dealt with as news to be reported, especially if you do not have a daily newspaper? Are they handled in a manner similar to the news media outside the school? How would you deal with a bomb threat that demanded the evacuation of the school?

INVESTIGATE

1   PHONE or VISIT your local radio or TV station and ask the news director how he receives and reports a fast-breaking news story in your immediate area, for instance, a fire, a serious auto accident.

2   Computerized projection allows the networks to declare political winners within hours of the polls' closing. Fast results of East Coast voting is said to affect last-minute voting on the West Coast. Are there other examples of instant news affecting decisions in the East-West time lag?

3   A large newspaper like the New York Times has newspapermen preparing obituaries for instant publication in the event of the sudden death of a public figure. CHECK your local news media to determine what preparations they make for a sudden major news break.

The story is told of a famous California publisher who became increasingly irritated because his Washington correspondents were being scooped by a nationally syndicated columnist who seemed to have an inside track. The publisher flew to the capital to confront the columnist, charged him with bribery, and insisted that he must be paying government officials to leak valuable information to him ahead of the regular press corps. The columnist denied the charge and pointed to several books on his desk, assignments for a course in nuclear physics. "Your men aren't well enough informed to ask the right questions," he maintained. "I wait until the general press conference is over, then ask my questions because I don't see why everyone should benefit from my doing my homework. I've studied military science, nuclear physics, economics, and foreign policy so I can ask the right questions. The admirals, cabinet members, and advisers are willing to answer if the reporter only knows what to ask."

 **THE RIGHT QUESTION**

Select a specialized information area from those listed below or one of your own choosing. Pick an area that you are especially well informed about, then match yourself with someone who admits he is not well informed in this particular area. Each of you prepare a list of five questions for an interview with an acknowledged expert in the area of your choice.

Special Area	Acknowledged Expert
Space program	Example: Director of NASA
Current authors	
Civil rights	
Basketball	
Football	
Motion pictures	
Women's styles	
State politics	
Military science	
Golf	

List both sets of questions below:

My questions: _____'s questions:

1   1

2   2

3   3

4   4

5   5

In what ways do the two lists of questions differ in:

Vocabulary?

Conciseness?

Purpose or Direction?

Other?

Does specialized background knowledge
influence the kind of questions the interviewer asks?

Estimate the relative value of the information to be gained from each set of questions.

Professional journalists today are not only
expected to be trained writers but also
knowledgeable specialists. For example:
What experience do you expect of someone covering the Republican or Democratic
National Conventions? A national woman's
lib meeting?

What education do you expect of a reporter
writing the Associated Press copy from
Cape Kennedy or the Houston Space Center?

What special education and/or experience
would you expect of the NBC correspondent
in Moscow?

What special experience would you expect
of an urban reporter covering the inner
city?

Which do you think would be more
important for the professional newsman: to develop expertise in a news
specialty? Or, to develop sensitivity
to sources, critical thinking skills,
and effective communication skill?

INTERFACE

How many of the reporting jobs mentioned above could you under-
take tomorrow?

Indicate below how you would recommend yourself to an editor in order to secure a job reporting in an area of your special competence.

Search out several examples of news stories in which the reporter obviously had to have specialized knowledge, experience, or background information in order to meet the challenge of the news event. (See if you can find two news reports on the same event that indicate that one reporter had specialized background and the other did not.)

Do any reporters for your school news media stay with one special assignment area through the school year?

Can you name newsmen that you follow regularly whom you respect for their experience and knowledge in a specialized area of news reporting?

INVESTIGATE

1   EXAMINE and evaluate the newsmen in your area for their specialized backgrounds. Are there political specialists? Science specialists? Sports experts? Business and economics specialists? Urban affairs specialists? Arts? Education?

2   ANALYZE several of the television talk show hosts. Do these men make some interviews more interesting than others because of their experience, education, or "homework" in certain areas? Or is the popular interviewer the one who directs most of his questions around his own interests and competences which are somehow similar to those of his audience?

3   If there is a school of journalism in your area, DISCUSS the education of newsmen with a member of the school faculty. Do they encourage future newsmen to develop a second major other than journalism?

One of the serious difficulties in international news gathering is the shortage of veteran reporters who stay on a foreign-service assignment long enough to become thoroughly acquainted with the key sources of news.

On the home front a similar difficulty can arise out of competition for news. Under pressure to produce a story or faced with a deadline, a reporter may sometimes settle for secondary or questionable or even fictionalized sources in preparing his copy.

Some news sources are clearly better than others. Some people are more knowledgeable, more credible, better qualified to comment on a situation than others. In short, the better the source, the better the news. This lab attempts to evaluate the quality of a news story in terms of the quality of its sources.

 NEWS SOURCE

As you read the two articles which follow from Newsweek and the New York Times, pick out and circle with a marking pen all the information derived from specific sources, identified or unidentified.

Next, reread the material you circled, underline the sources cited, and evaluate each source according to the rating scale given below.

Finally, tally the scores for each article and compare them.

Example: Newsweek

"If this were a secret vote on a House resolution showing contempt for the media," said one Democrat later, "the vote would be 420-15--or worse."

The Selling of Congress

For the second time in a fortnight, the powers of the government and the freedom of the press seemed bound for a head-on legal collision last week—and then, at the last moment, swerved into a relatively mild sideswipe. The House of Representatives had appeared to be driving toward a contempt citation against CBS for refusing to hand over unused portions of its controversial television documentary "The Selling of the Pentagon." Then, Congressional leaders of both parties grew leery of putting the constitutional issues to a clear-cut test. The White House, too, lost its taste for another assault on the media so soon after its futile effort to suppress the Pentagon papers. And in the end, the House gently shelved the whole sticky affair.

The network clearly had the better of the encounter—it was the first time the House had failed to back up one of its committees in a case of contempt, and it implied that the media are more immune than others to Congressional investigation. But the only unqualified victor in the affair seemed to be the old rule of American politics that in a clash of principle between two respected causes, the issue is better left hanging than resolved. The only loser was a stubborn West Virginian who had sought to defy that tradition, the chairman of the House Interstate and Foreign Commerce Committee, Harley O. Staggers.

Declined: From the moment that CBS president Frank Stanton declined to honor his committee's subpoena last month, Staggers had pressed for a vote of contempt. To him, the issue was straightforward: his committee was investigating "The Selling of the Pentagon" to decide whether to propose legislation banning deceitful editorial devices such as some thought had been used in making this show; the CBS "outtakes" were relevant to that investigation; CBS had refused to furnish them; therefore the network was in contempt of Congress. At issue, in this view, was Congress's right to obtain information needed in making laws.

CBS, on the other hand, saw it as a First Amendment issue. The Constitution forbids Congress from making laws abridging the freedom of the press. To submit a show's outtakes—the film that is not used in its final edited version—would be to submit the editorial process to legislative scrutiny, the network argued, and. this would inevitably produce a "chilling" effect on the newsman's freedom to present the news without government interference.

Realities: Both CBS's and Staggers's arguments, however, were somewhat shaky. The broadcasters' claim to an untrammeled First Amendment right to air what they please collides with one reality: the limited number of channels makes some government regulation inevitable. As a matter of fact,

certain restrictive laws—such as the "equal time" provision and the rules against quiz-show rigging—are already in force and have been generally approved by the Supreme Court. And Staggers could not fully establish that the CBS outtakes were essential to his investigation because the most crucial information they contained had already been given to the committee by other sources.

Given the high stakes and the legal uncertainties, a number of Staggers's colleagues tried to head him off. "Harley," Massachusetts Democrat Turbert MacDonald, a trusted fellow committeeman, urged several weeks ago, "apply the George Aiken principle on Vietnam to this issue: run up the flag, declare a victory—and get out of it." MacDonald, along with an increasing number of congressmen, was worried about the implications of defeat. "The networks can be arrogant as it is," he said, "but if this thing went to the Supreme Court and we lost, they would be incorrigible." But Staggers couldn't be budged, and a week before the vote he sent MacDonald to the House leadership to request a head count of the Democrats. Very reluctantly, Speaker Carl Albert agreed. The totals showed 91 members opposed to the contempt citation, 71 in favor and 93 undecided. The leaders interpreted the 93 don't-knows as evidence of a strong desire to finesse the issue, but Staggers regarded

---

Media Score Card -- Sources

+5   Identified source with well known qualifications, background, involvement in the event.

+2   Identified source with less qualification, background, or involvement on this topic.

0   Information attributed to a source who is not known to be qualified or involved in this event. Also information coming from "informed sources" which may be suspect or questionable because there is no way to tell who they are.

-3   Unidentified source, or information from vaguely identified source, "one Democrat said." If the information is distorted or out of context, nobody can affirm or deny it. There is no way to evaluate this source.

them as ripe for conversion. Besides, he was convinced that any Democratic deficiency would be more than overcome by Republicans.

He seemed to have good reason for optimism. William Springer of Illinois, Commerce's ranking GOP member, was backing the contempt citation just as enthusiastically as Staggers. In addition, Staggers had sent an emissary to Minority Leader Gerald Ford and got back word, two weeks ago, that Ford would support them. But as a matter of fact, Ford was growing ever more wary of the project, very largely as a result of the Supreme Court's ruling on the Pentagon papers. And he spotted a serious political hazard for the Administration. "If the committee citation had succeeded," one of Ford's intimates pointed out later, "it would have put the President and the Justice Department in the embarrassing position of having to prosecute this thing, and we'd be right back as the big, bad Administration persecuting the press." This same warning was quietly circulated by White House liaison men, and as the vote approached, a check by Republicans indicated that the GOP members, far from offering the citation overwhelming support, were split about 50-50.

Tide: One day before the vote, Staggers got his first serious inkling that the tide had turned against him. Wilbur Mills, the influential chairman of the House Ways and Means Committee, put out word that he was "troubled" by the contempt citation and would not support it. Staggers had been counting on a solid front of committee chairmen on his side—contempt citations have traditionally been passed almost as a matter of the chairman's personal privilege—and Mills's defection hurt. In the end, six of his fellow chairmen voted against him.

A few hours before voting was to begin, Staggers was jolted with worse news: Albert wanted to send the citation back to committee and—adding sting to the slap—to the Judiciary Committee, not Commerce. He rushed to the Speaker's chambers, and for a moment the two normally mild men paired off in an angry shouting match. "I don't need the leadership," Staggers stormed. "If you give me my hour, I can convince the House that this is the right thing to do." "Harley," said Democratic Whip Thomas P. (Tip) O'Neill Jr., "you haven't got a chance."

Bill Springer, meanwhile, was hearing the same grim message on the Republican side of the aisle: suddenly, he reported, "everybody in the leadership was talking about a motion to recommit." Staggers got his hour of debate. Few kind things were said about CBS or television in general. "If this were a secret vote on a House resolution showing contempt for the media," said one Democrat later, "the vote would be 420-15—or worse." But if the average congressman feels bedeviled by the media, he also feels beholden to them come election time—and CBS's local affiliates (many of which acutely disliked the Pentagon show) had mounted an effective lobbying campaign on the network's behalf.

Tenderness: High principles were not, however, ignored. "The First Amendment towers over these proceedings like a colossus," declared Emmanuel Celler, the chairman of Judiciary, "and no esprit de corps and no tenderness of one member for another should force us to topple over this monument to our liberties." Tenderness did lead the House to cushion the rebuke to Staggers as much as possible. The contempt citation was not rejected but recommitted—and to Commerce, not Judiciary—but everyone, Staggers included, knew it was dead. The vote was 226-181; in both parties, there was a majority to recommit.

"Lord, I'm disappointed," sighed Staggers as he left the floor. In New York, CBS's Stanton happily hailed "the decisive House vote." It remains to be seen just how decisive the vote may have been. Two days afterward, Massachusetts Republican Hastings Keith, who had introduced the motion to recommit, filed a truth-in-broadcasting bill that would require TV programs, he said, "to advise their audiences when an apparent 'news happening' really is a staged happening; when an apparent 'spontaneous, unrehearsed interview' really is not; and when a taped or filmed interview has been altered." Staggers himself is likely to introduce a similar bill after the Congressional vacation next month. The showdown that Congress avoided last week may simply have been postponed.

Newsweek
July 26, 1971

Newsweek tally:

N. Y. Times

C. B. S. & Congress:

The Shelling Of the Pentagon

WASHINGTON — Two weeks ago, Congressman Harley Staggers of West Virginia, who heads a subcommittee that investigates network misdeeds, was convinced he had the Columbia Broadcasting System against the wall.

Back in those happy days he was assuring colleagues and reporters that the House of Representatives would surely hold C.B.S. President Frank Stanton in contempt for refusing to surrender all the film taken in the production of the documentary "The Selling of the Pentagon"—a show that Mr. Staggers felt had been edited with the intent to deceive the public.

There was good reason for Mr. Staggers to feel confident. Not for many years had the House turned down a properly transmitted request for a contempt citation. And in this instance the offending party's position seemed all the more perilous because "The Selling of the Pentagon," which criticized and ridiculed the military's costly public relations program, had not set well with the Pentagon's friends, who probably constitute a majority in the House.

Nevertheless, when the showdown came last week, C.B.S. won. By a vote of 226 to 181, the House refused to consider the contempt proposal and instead sent it back to Mr. Staggers' Commerce committee for burial.

How did it happen? Mr. Staggers could not have chosen a more awkward time to fight with the network. The air was still filled with freedom-of-the-press bunting, after the celebrated Supreme Court ruling that the Government should keep its hand out of editorial matters and that The New York Times and The Washington Post could continue publishing the Pentagon Papers. The decision seemed to please large segments of the public, and Congressmen are quick to notice such things. Another element of bad timing on Mr. Staggers' part was that after 1971 comes 1972, and in Presidential years it is nice to have the networks as friends. Some believe it was for this reason only that Mr. Staggers lost the vote of Wilbur Mills, whose customary stubborn defense of House traditions may have been modified by faint stirrings of Presidential ambitions.

And not to withhold credit where due, there is a constant band of members—the likes of such lawyers as Emanuel Celler of New York and Robert Eckhardt of Texas—who can argue very eloquently for the Bill of Rights. Who is to say but that on some rare occasions other members listen and are persuaded?

But Mr. Staggers and his allies had another explanation for their defeat: A lobbying campaign such as they had never seen before which reached the peak of its intensity on the eve and on the day of the vote. C.B.S. men had been walking the halls of the House Office Building for weeks, they said, as had the National Association of Broadcasters' 50-man "Future of Broadcasting Committee."

C.B.S.'s lawyers indicated a concern that if the corporation had to take the contempt citation to court, it might lose. There was no assurance that the courts would see it as a First Amendment issue, since it is not clear that the First Amendment fully covers the networks as it does the newspapers. So C.B.S. allegedly went all out to prevent the citation from clearing the House.

Representative William L. Springer of Illinois, ranking Republican on the Interstate and Foreign Commerce Committee, which oversees network affairs, said, "I must have personally talked to between 60 and 80 Republicans who ran to me and asked what the hell was going on. They all had been

Media Score Card -- Sources

+5   Identified source with well known qualifications, background, involvement in the event.

+2   Identified source with less qualification, background, or involvement on this topic.

0   Information attributed to a source who is not known to be qualified or involved in this event. Also information coming from "informed sources" which may be suspect or questionable because there is no way to tell who they are.

−3   Unidentified source, or information from vaguely identified source, "one Democrat said." If the information is distorted or out of context, nobody can affirm or deny it. There is no way to evaluate this source.

contacted, most of them several times, by TV and radio station people. One member told me he had had 13 contacts. I haven't seen anything like this in 21 years." (After the vote, Mr. Staggers went around waving TV Digest and urging everyone to "Read it, read it." TV Digest has described the lobbying as "fierce.")

One House member told of a TV station owner in his district who had threatened to drive him out of office if he voted with Mr. Staggers. So he didn't. Another said his hometown's C.B.S. station was already giving generous time to a young man who had just a few days earlier announced to run against him. An important Democratic supporter of the anti-C.B.S. resolution said, "I was made keenly aware, through numerous phone calls from industry people, that if I persisted in my present course, there would be a number of useful and valuable relationships that would change."

Another who asked not to be identified because "I've got to live with these people" said that, as the lobbying drive entered the homestretch, "The manager of my local television station called me twice, the manager of the biggest radio station in Michigan called once, the Michigan Association of Broadcasters wrote letters, a local newspaper editor who said he had been encouraged by C.B.S. to do so gave

me a call, and finally, I was contacted by a lobbyist I've known for years. He told me he had been hired by C.B.S. lawyers to see if he couldn't win me over. It wasn't very subtle."

Many on the losing side agreed with Mr. Springer, who accused Mr. Stanton of "being right in the middle" of the pressure campaign and of making numerous personal phone calls to the Democratic and Republican leadership "right up to the day of the vote."

Indeed, something did seem to have happened to the leadership as the time for the vote approached. Mr. Staggers had told friends that as a result of several conferences with Speaker Carl Albert and Democratic Whip Hale Boggs, he felt he had their tacit approval. (At least they hadn't tried to convince him that he was heading for an embarrassing defeat.) Republican leader Gerald R. Ford was said to have promised several on his side, including Mr. Springer, that he would support the citation. One frustrated anti-C.B.S. Republican swore, "Fifteen minutes before the vote, you goddamn betcha, Jerry told me he was still with us. And when the going got rough, Jerry finked. He ran, and so did Carl, and so did Boggs. Oh hell, they ran like rats around here. We would have won if it hadn't been for such tough lobbying."

Among those in C.B.S.'s pay and among those who felt that a vote for C.B.S. was a vote for the Constitution, such complaints of being pressured too much were dismissed as hysterical and unfair. A spokesman for C.B.S.'s Washington counsel, Wilmer, Cutler & Pickering, acknowledged that several members of the firm had been busy on the case and that he himself had talked to a few Congressmen, "convincingly in a couple of cases, I like to think." But he was distressed to hear it called lobbying. "We were just giving our legal opinion. If you want good lobbyists," he said, "you don't come to us. We are very poor at that."

As for what Mr. Stanton would respond to specific charges of heavy-handed lobbying, that is something that must be left to another day, for at present he refuses to submit to direct questioning on these points. Instead he issued a general statement which read, in part, "It would have been inappropriate in my judgment for C.B.S. to have solicited among our affiliates an all-out campaign to persuade Congress that the contempt citation was not in the public interest, and therefore we did not." The help C.B.S. had received, he wrote, was "voluntary."

—ROBERT SHERRILL
Mr. Sherrill is a free-lance writer based in Washington.

New <u>York</u> <u>Times</u> tally:

 **COMPARE AND EVALUATE**

Use the Media Score Card given above and apply it to two accounts of the same news story as covered by two different media, newspaper and news magazine, or two different newspapers, or a newspaper and a TV news report.

Do you think this scoring method is a fair way to judge the credibility of a news story?

There is real news value in a direct quotation from an obviously knowledgeable and reliable source, but sometimes a reporter must protect or shield his source. How much does the reader depend on the reliability of the reporter and the reputation of the journal which carries the story?

In a signed news report, how much credit will you give to unidentified sources whose names are withheld to protect them?

In a signed news report, how much credit will you give to identified sources who later deny that they made such a statement?

> It is part of an investigative reporter's code never to divulge his sources of information without their permission. The juicier the tip, the more the informant usually needs this protection. Without it, he'd keep his knowledge to himself. If it became impossible for reporters to protect the anonymity of informants, confidential news tips would dry up. The free press, as we have known it at its best, investigating corruption and protecting the public interest, would cease to exist. RICHARD FRISBIE

INTERFACE

Rumors are a popular form of information flow. Do you normally question the source of a rumor? Do you normally check out its accuracy with the person who is supposed to have started it?

Make a Media Score Card evaluation on a recent bulletin in your school. How clear is the accountability for statements made there?

INVESTIGATE

1   INTERVIEW a reporter who has recently covered a major news event that attracted a large number of reporters. Ask him about the difficulty of getting cooperation from news sources when there are many reporters trying to get the story. Ask him about the value and use of the news pool that John Linstead mentions in his article about Attica.

2   CALL several of your local news media and inquire what their chief news sources are. Do television stations use newspapers? Do newspapers use television news reports? Who uses the wire services? How many original reporters do they have?

3   The credibility of news sources can make major news itself. In 1972 there was the bogus autobiography of Howard Hughes by Clifford Irving and the ITT memo reported by Jack Anderson. REVIEW these news stories or a current controversy and evaluate the public's reaction to the credibility of the news sources.

Reporters are often assigned to a beat; they cover the courts, city hall, the ball park, or the police beat. Many larger newspapers and broadcast stations have specialty editors and reporters.

Once a newsman has learned his beat or frequently covered a certain type of story there is a persistent danger that he will unwittingly program himself into "story type 101." Like the annual prom story in the school newspaper, the reporter may use the same story outline and just fill in new names, dates, and places. The reporter who gets used to his beat may come with his expectancy levels too high and miss the unique quality of the event, the human interest element that can make all the difference; or he may just overlook the angle that can make for a more significant news story.

LAB   DO-IT-YOURSELF PROTEST REPORT

Write your own protest demonstration report by filling in the numbered blanks from the corresponding numbered lists.

.............[1]............. paraded through ....[2].........

in ....[3]............today protesting ....[4]...........

The demonstration began after ......[5]...... was ....[6].........

by ....[7]...........

When police arrived they were greeted by a shower of ....[8]........ and

shouts of ....[9].......... The police responded ....[10]........

Speaking over television, this evening, the Governor declared......[11]......

and called.........[12].........

Read your sample reports out loud to the class. Do the programmed sentences make sense?

1	2	3	4
500 Yippies	the streets	Berkeley	the war in Vietnam
Black militants	the suburbs	Chicago	school bussing
Shouting students	a back alley	Detroit	higher taxes
Three acid heads	a vacant lot	Greenwich Village	slumlords
Angry mothers	the sewers	Haight-Ashbury	the Supreme Court
Right-wing extremists	their living rooms	boredom	marriage
Underpaid teachers	the girl's dorm	anger	divorce
Overpaid teachers	the Dean's office	the nude	dirty magazines
Enraged Maoists	a revolving door	new Spring hats	freedom of speech
An old maid	a phone booth	confusion	dirty movies
A bunch of nuts	the YMCA	single file	baths
	Harry's Diner		this article

5	6	7	8
a bearded male	seized	an off-duty policeman	rocks
a moustached female	denounced	the S.D.S.	obscenities
a homemade bomb	suppressed	a Senate Committee	manhole covers
a Viet Cong flag	attacked	a CBS News Team	abuse
a C.I.A. agent	beaten	counter demonstrators	insults
a dope pusher	obliterated	advocates of free love	bananas
Eldridge Cleaver	arrested	the Mayor	praise
Mod Squad	applauded	the Governor	pizza crusts
Dr. Timothy Leary	put on probation	the President	mandalas
a picketing cabbie	hugged and kissed	angry in-laws	old Nixon buttons
"MAD Magazine"	ignored	proxy	flowers
		mistake	rain

9	10	11	12
"Make love, not war!"	with nightsticks	a state of emergency	for calm
"Make war, not love!"	with tear gas	a cooling-off period	for help
"Hell no, we won't go!"	with mass arrests	that he was quitting	up the National Guard
"Draft beer, not students!"	by ducking	a new holiday	for an investigation
"Burn, baby, burn!"	in kind	an extra dividend	Dial-a-Prayer
"Fascist pigs!"	with a big hello	that he was uptight	for his pipe and slippers
"Nixon was the one!"	by refusing to listen	the sky was falling	out for sandwiches
"Commie cruds!"	with a song	that he was unfit	for higher taxes
"We love Mayor Daley!"	by yelling back	a day of mourning	for equal time
"Up against the wall!"	with snappy stories	he was a new grandfather	everybody names
"Walt Disney lives!"	by retreating	bankruptcy	for sweeping changes
"Sock it to me!"	by resigning	war	his mother

171

 STANDARD PATTERNS

See if you can find examples of news reports that follow a standard pattern. Collect several of these stories and underline the elements they have in common. Select one of these stories that shows distinct signs of being "stock" or programmed reporting and duplicate it for class analysis.

Does the story compare or contrast this news event with other similar news events?

Does the story point out the unique characteristics of this news event?

Does the story quote the obvious news sources normally associated with this kind of news event, or does it cite a variety of sources, some unexpected?

If you were assigned to cover this event, how would you proceed differently?

INTERFACE

Have you ever established a formula for doing your assignments or for doing research papers that's fast, efficient, and a convenient way to dispatch the responsibility? If so, comment on the quality of the writing, its readability.

If you have ever had a close friend who has made the news, have you ever been surprised at the way reporters have represented him? Were their descriptions adequate or inadequate? Why?

INVESTIGATE

1 COMPARE sports reports on the same game in several different newspapers and analyze the similarities and differences. Some sports copy is written from wire service box scores by staff writers who have not seen the game. Is there any evidence of this practice in your area?

2 PREPARE your own "Do-It-Yourself" newspaper story based on stories from a "high expectation" news area.

3 FIND out how many reporters in your area have regular news beats. What are the beats? Ask the reporters whether they think news beats make them more susceptible to the dangers of programmed reporting.

4 EVALUATE your school newspaper for programmed reporting.

5 DEVELOP an exhibit of outstanding news stories in which the newsmen, as far as you can tell, turned routine stories into unique pieces of reporting.

In 1962 when Richard Nixon was defeated in his bid for governor of California, just two years after his loss to John F. Kennedy in his first bid for the presidency, he said to the members of the press, "Well, you won't have Nixon to kick around any more." Yet Nixon returned to political life and like all political figures went on dealing with newsmen.

The relationship between a public figure and a newsman is often critical in determining how much information the public will receive on a given topic. The public figure has the power to release or withhold information that the news media wants. The newsman has the power to build up or injure a man's public image. There is a tension here, sometimes a power struggle, sometimes a mutual trust, and sometimes a favoritism to one reporter rather than another.

In any case, newsmakers have not been known to talk to reporters the way they talk with their intimate friends. This fact has implications for all of us in the news audience, and it is one to explore in the following lab.

 PERSON-TO-PERSON

Simulate a series of interviews as indicated below based on the following news situation.

The administration, school board, and parent organization of Thomas Jefferson High School have received many complaints about student abuse of the school parking lot. The lot is directly across the street from a grade school and cars have been reported leaving the lot at speeds in excess of forty miles per hour. Some students actually drag race in the parking lot. Students leave the school to use their cars for smoking, eating, and unexcused trips from the campus. Faculty members complain that their reserved spaces are often filled.

The principal acting with a parent committee has just issued new student parking regulations. Only cars with approved stickers will be allowed in the parking lot. These stickers will only be given to students who can show serious cause for driving to school and needing the parking lot. For example, physical disability, activities commitments that keep the student late after school, or a special parent request which will be evaluated by a parent-faculty committee.

The new parking regulations have caused unfavorable student reaction. Reporters from the following news media are seeking interviews with the principal.

The Jeffersonian, the weekly school newspaper

The Outrider, an alternate student newspaper printed on a secondhand
duplicator, appears about twice a month

The Middletown Times, a daily paper which virtually every family in the
town subscribes to

School District Newsletter, published weekly by the public communications
director who prepares press releases for the local news media

The principal calls the president of the parent committee and asks him to sit in on each of the interviews. At the end of the last interview, the two talk about what happened.

Six people in the class can volunteer to play the roles of the principal, the president of the parent committee, the three reporters, and the communications director. Each reporter should conduct his interview separately from the other three and not be present in the classroom for the other interviews. The principal controls the length of time he will allow each reporter, but the maximum should be ten minutes. He may also deny an interview to any or all of the reporters; but if they request it, he should be prepared to give a reason for his denial.

Principal:

Parent Committee President:

Jeffersonian reporter:

Outrider reporter:

Times reporter:

District Newsletter publisher:

When the interviews and the discussion with the president of the parent committee are completed, evaluate the quality of the interviews and the relationships between the parties on a scale from one to ten. One--interview denied, or was closed, uncooperative, defensive, or evasive. Ten--interview was open, cooperative, with free flow of information.

Jeffersonian

Outrider

Times

Newsletter

Parent Committee President

If the principal favored some reporters with more information and cooperation than others, why did he do so?

Do you normally evaluate a news source in terms of his past relationship with the news media? Should this be a basis for your evaluating a news story?

How important is the relationship between the reporter and the news source for getting at the whole truth?

Do you think it is normal for a person to try to control the newsman who will be writing about him?

Some newsmen and news media are denied credentials to news conferences with public officials. Do you see practical reasons for credentialing reporters? Do you approve of it?

What training would you recommend for newsmen to help them maintain good relations with their sources?

INTERFACE

Have you ever been interviewed for a story you knew would appear in the news? How did you feel? Did you trust the reporter to represent you fairly, accurately, and in context?

When you see ordinary people being interviewed on television, do you ever put yourself in their place? Do you think such persons tend to be defensive, or are they too open?

Do you find that some broadcast interviewers are better able to create a natural flow of information than others? If so, cite examples and explain how they accomplish this?

Of all the television news reporters and talk show interviewers you can think of, which one would you prefer to have interview you? Which one would you least like to have interview you?

INVESTIGATE

1   INTERVIEW local newsmen to find out whether their education as newsmen included human relations and inter-personal communications training. Do they see these skills as necessary to their work?

2   Presidential press conferences began with Franklin D. Roosevelt. EVALUATE the relationship of recent presidents with the Washington press corps. Has television changed these relationships?

Where I Stand -

Based on your experience with the units in this section, which of the following positions seems better to you?

a) Since the information media are faced with so many limitations and truth is so hard to get at, we have to resign ourselves to making decisions based on very uncertain data.

b) Once we are aware of the human factors and limitations that make the communication of truth so difficult, we can make critical judgments about our information sources that will generally improve the quality of our decisions.

SIMULATE

Using the insights and conclusions you arrived at above, role play the following Media Man Simulation.

You are the city editor of a metropolitan daily paper. A controversial revolutionary is going to speak on a local college campus this evening. You have two reporters who could cover the assignment. One is liberal, has good relations with youth groups, and speaks the language of the revolutionary culture. The other is a more experienced reporter, more reserved in his politics, and a persevering interviewer, even though he does not always endear himself to others. Which reporter will you send?

Editing and Ownership

From the vast potential for news, a series of decisions made by an editor results in few relatively incomplete news stories reaching the reader, listener or viewer. Each reporter and editor along the path from the news event to the consumer is like a gatekeeper who controls the flow of news.

JAMES K. BUCKALEW

In making their selection, newsmen also apply values, most of which are professional . . . and a few of which are personal. Newsmen prefer stories that report people rather than social processes.

HERBERT J. GANS

The activities of public relations men often are constructive. . . . But the vast public relations apparatus is not provided by government and industry out of pure altruism. The public relations man's duty to his employer or client is to further a certain point of view. The discerning reader will be aware of this and allow for it as an important influence in the news.

RICHARD FRISBIE

Whatever the skills and competence of a newsman, he knows that the story he files is always subject to the relay process that goes on within his medium.

The newsman begins the process with his typewritten copy, his phone call, his film, tape recording, cablegram, or satellite transmission. He rarely controls the fate of his news material beyond that point unless he has the power of a Harry Reasoner or that of a major columnist like Irving Sablonsky.

In order for the newsman's story to reach the mass audience, it must go through relay processes which alter his original story. So there is an advantage for the people, the news consumers, to have some idea of how the process works.

 NEWS RELAY TEAM

In this lab the class will simulate an actual news relay process.

Set up a news conference interview on an important local news story. Invite someone vitally linked to that story to appear for the press conference.

Five members of the class will act as reporters and it will be their responsibility to ask the right questions and keep the press conference moving. Four other members of the class will be rewrite men. And another five will be editors. The rewrite men and editors, of course, will not attend the press conference. The remaining members of the class can join in the press conference with the reporters.

Reporter A: _____ for the Evening Times has to meet an afternoon deadline.

Reporter B: _____ for the City News Bureau wants to get his report on the wires as soon as possible.

Reporter C: _____ for KLCN radio wants to make the next hourly news report.

Reporter D: _____ for the Daily News, a morning paper, has until 10 p.m. to file his story.

Reporter E: _____ for a weekly news magazine, has more time to write and file his story.

Step One: As soon as possible after the press conference, reporters A, B, and C phone their reports to their rewrite men. (Tape recordings of the reports will be helpful for later analysis.) Reporters D and E write their stories.

Step Two: Relay-rewrite men prepare written copy to be printed or broadcast.

Rewrite Man A: _____ at the Evening Times receives the call from Reporter A, asks questions to clear up points and get all the facts of the story. Allowing himself only one hour, he composes the story. The editor has asked for a 250-word story.

Rewrite Man B: _____ at the City News Bureau takes phone report from Reporter B and proceeds to write the story. He makes word-length decision based on his own estimate of the story's importance.

Copy Editor C: _____ at KLCN radio tape records phone report from Reporter C so he can use direct sound report on the air. He writes copy and decides what parts, if any, to play "live" on a 40-second newscast.

Rewrite Man D: _____ at the Daily News accepts written copy from Reporter D, discusses it with him, and edits the copy for publication. He allows himself one hour writing time for a 450-word slot.

Step Three: Editors and news directors make final decisions on news copy.

Bureau Chief B: _____ at City News Bureau accepts copy from Rewrite Man B and decides how much of it will be put on the City News wire. (This copy should be duplicated and distributed immediately to the following four editors and the class.)

City Editor A: _____ at the Evening Times accepts copy from Rewrite Man A. He may call the reporter and ask additional questions or make suggestions about the story. He decides how much of the story he will print. He also receives the wire service copy and may decide to use it instead of his own, or he may ask that his own copy be rewritten to include information in the wire copy.

News Director C: _____ at KLCN accepts copy and tape from his Copy Editor, reviews the wire service copy, then broadcasts on tape the 40-second news report.

City Editor D: _____ receives copy from Rewrite Man D as well as the wire service copy. He proceeds in the same way as City Editor A above.

Managing Editor E: _____ at the weekly news magazine accepts copy directly from Reporter E, discusses it with him for possible revision, and reviews the stories already published by the wire service, the Times, the Daily News, and the KLCN newscast.

<u>Step Four</u>: All four print media provide copies of their completed news reports for the class. KLCN offers its radio tape.

Ask each of the news teams to describe what happened from the press conference through the finished news stories.

Use the space below to draw a model of the relay process each story passed through before it reached its final form.

Story A:

Story B:

Story C:

Story D:

Story E:

<u>Step Five</u>: As you listen to the news teams and review their finished stories, complete the following evaluation sheet on the effects of the relay-editing process. Ratings: Y--Yes, in a major way. N--No, not significantly. S--Somewhat.

Story	A	B	C	D	E
1 Did the facts of the story change?					
2 Were facts lost or garbled in the relay process?					
3 Were facts restored or clarified in the relay process?					
4 Did the emphasis of the story shift?					
5 Did the pressure of time affect the accuracy of the story?					

FOCUS

If you were present at the original press conference, which finished story did you find most accurate and informative?

Which accounts did you find satisfactory, given the pressure of time and the limits of the medium?

Do you think any account was harmed in the relay-editing process?

What kinds of changes were made by those who were not present at the press conference? Were they helpful or not?

Flora Lewis, nationally syndicated columnist, points up some of the changes that might occur in a news report when the film or videotape is edited.

TV techniques raise questions

By Flora Lewis

NEW YORK—Although CBS president Frank Stanton won his adamant stand against a congressional demand for unused film, some needed soul-searching is beginning among electronic newsmen.

Some new guidelines have been issued for documentary films after the controversy over "The Selling of the Pentagon." New guidelines have been issued on news interviews, too, a result of complaints from Lyndon B. Johnson after his series with Walter Cronkite.

Cronkite conducted 30 hours of filmed interviews with the former President, for which Mr. Johnson was lavishly paid. It was compressed into three hours, with questions eliminated when various answers seemed to fit conveniently under a single heading. Mr. Johnson complained about that and about "reverse shots," separate shots of Cronkite repeating his questions for the camera when Mr. Johnson was not there.

The President charged, "I think unfairly," Cronkite said, "that I changed my facial expression to show doubts. I don't think I did." Still, the Columbia Broadcasting System has ruled against the "reverse shots" in future, unless they are unavoidable because there is only one camera available and it can't film the interviewer and the interviewee at the same time.

This matters because it spotlights the question of television techniques, which Rep. Harley O. Staggers (D-W. Va.) said was the point of his effort to have CBS held in contempt of Congress for refusing to turn over its unedited film.

IN THE EMOTION generated over "The Selling of the Pentagon" fuss, two issues that ought to be distinct were unfortunately blurred. One is ethical, technical and professional. The other is constitutional.

Reports from both sides have made it appear that the question was whether the First Amendment guaranteeing freedom of speech and of the press means television can operate as it pleases. Quite rightly, Staggers said that would be intolerable, given the enormous power of television. But that was not the question.

The refusal of the House to vote CBS in contempt upheld the essential principle that the First Amendment does apply to television. The Supreme Court already had ruled that in the case of the press, unpublished material cannot be subpoenaed. The House action now implies that this ruling also covers television.

I doubt anybody involved with gathering and presenting news would disagree with that. The work should be judged by the results, and it would be practically impossible to write, film and edit with the knowledge that Congress or the courts were going to second-guess false starts, rejects and editorial judgment.

But there is another question about television techniques that has developed with the new medium. Television APPEARS to show just what happened, even if only a brief slice of what happened.

But it often doesn't. Splices, reverse shots, invisible cuts are regularly used to reduce running time and still give a sense of continuity. It is, argue TV men, no different from what newspapermen do in transforming a jumble of information and impressions into print.

AS CRONKITE POINTS OUT, printed stories often fail even to note that questions were asked, making it sound that quoted remarks were volunteered instead of given in reply to what may have been a provocative or even double-edged question.

"It's true this technique (TV) is susceptible to sleazy practice," Cronkite told me. "All our techniques are. We have the freedom to be wrong or sleazy, but responsible journalists are not. We're trying to do an honest reportorial job. I don't see how you can do this without editing."

Cronkite, as conscientious and honest a journalist as this country has produced, nonetheless misses something, I think. It is that the viewer is led to believe he is watching the equivalent of a text, unaware of any tinkering.

Television is here to stay. It is time for its professionals to review their techniques, eschewing fakery and explaining to their audience where needed that TV, too, processes raw life.

Partly the trouble is in the eye of the beholder. Cronkite has long argued that there should be school courses in how to read a newspaper and how to watch television.

The public also needs some assurance of truth in packaging broadcasts, not by congressional harassment but by television's own improved standard of ethics.

Chicago Sun-Times
July 20, 1971

FOCUS

Are you aware that you don't always
view film in its actual time sequence?

As a viewer at home, is there any
way you can tell how film has been
edited?

INTERFACE

Have you ever been involved in a news event which was distorted
in the reporting-relay-editing process? What was your reaction?

In learning about social and political issues, how many relays stand
between you in the classroom and the actual events or realities?
What do you think about this relay system?

Do you think of live news coverage on television as "first hand"
experience? Are you aware of the television relay system?

INVESTIGATE

1   VISIT your local newspaper and interview a rewrite man to find out how he sees
his role in the news gathering operation. Would he rather cover stories as a reporter?

2   Courts have had to decide who is legally responsible for an error in a wire
service story, the wire service or the media which use their stories. INVESTIGATE
Wood vs. Constitution Publishing Company, 194 S.E. 760, 765 Georgia, 1937.

3   FIND OUT if a local newspaper, radio or television station would allow some
students to follow a local news story from beginning to end.

The Gatekeeper studies began back in the 1950's. Communication analysts were aware that the decisions made in a few key positions in a news room effectively determine what eventually appears in the paper or newscast. The Gatekeepers control the flow of news; they accept some stories and reject others. These editors determine how much "play" or emphasis each story will get. They decide the size of headlines, the time length and sequence of stories on the newscasts.

The first studies focused on the wire service editor. He screens hundreds of international, national, and regional stories off the teletype every day. Some he passes on to the managing editor, others he files in the wastebasket. In a small city daily that wire service copy often represents as much as half of the news copy in the paper. The studies sought to discover how the wire editor's decisions were influenced by his politics, religion, company policy, personal interests, and other factors.

Broadcast news also has its Gatekeepers. Most radio stations do not have a news staff large enough to produce their own on-the-hour newscasts. So the newscaster reads the five-minute (pretimed) summary provided by the wire service, probably the AP (Associated Press) or the UPI (United Press International). The man in the regional AP or UPI office who makes the hourly choice of stories for hundreds of stations is an influential Gatekeeper too. How does he decide?

The lab which follows is a simple probe into the function of the Gatekeeper.

LAB FACING THE GATEKEEPER

Your school allows a twenty minute TV newscast once a week on Friday afternoons. Have members of your class simulate the selection process for the telecast. Let one person be the news editor, another the sports editor. The other members of the class assume the role of news sources, each one assigned to a speciality area in the school. After uncovering a story with news value, the source people write brief copy and include suggestions for making the story visual.

The news editor and sports editor each sit in the middle of a fence of desks and admit the "source" students to the "Accepted area" of the classroom if they accept their stories for use on the telecast. These storymakers may be seated. If the editors reject a story, the storymaker has to remain standing outside the fence in the "Rejected area."

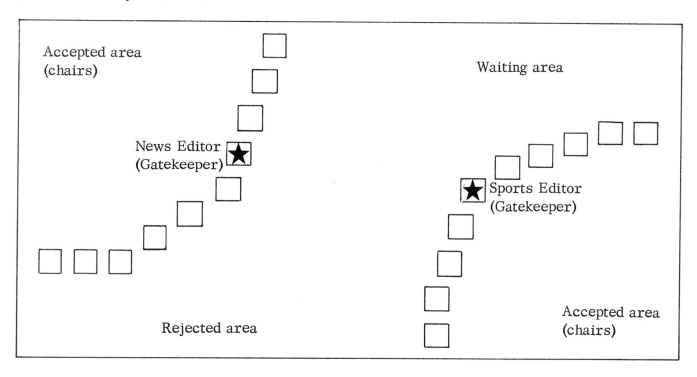

The editor must keep in mind the timing for the newscast which is determined as follows:

9 1/2 minutes	- news
4 minutes	- sports
(4 1/2 minutes	- advertisements and announcements from school organizations)
(2 minutes	- editorial comment or reply to previous comments)

When the last stories have been accepted or rejected, the Gatekeepers should answer questions from the class as to how and why they made their editorial decisions.

What criteria did the Gatekeepers use to
select or reject stories?

Which decisions might have been different
if the Gatekeepers were selecting news
stories for the school newspaper rather
than for television?

In what way, if any, did the Gatekeepers'
decisions reflect their own interests, concerns, and biases?

Influences like these—the emphasis on picture stories, the
lack of time and resources with which to make crucial
decisions, the pressures to "fill" the program, to conform
to what everyone else says is news, and the intrusion of
people with limited journalistic credentials or instincts into
the decision-making—shape the form and substance of TV
news every day.   RICHARD TOWNLEY

LAB   YOU ARE THE GATEKEEPER

As Editor of your local daily newspaper, you have space for seven stories off the wires (Associated Press and United Press International). These stories will fill the news space that remains open after the front page and local news stories have been chosen. The stories will appear in the afternoon home-delivery edition. The paper serves your geographic area. Which of the following stories would you select for those seven slots?

Check seven:

1 A British report on Soviet atom-missile build-up
2 Terrorists shoot at a guard depot in front of the U.S. embassy in Montevideo, Uruguay
3 Federal attorneys have been sent into Mississippi to assist school desegregation
4 Holiday traffic toll
5 Jacqueline Onassis returns to Greece from New York for holidays
6 Federal court indicts a major crime syndicate boss
7 Month-long projection of the weather
8 Threat of a senate filibuster on a women's rights bill
9 New safety features planned for next year's cars
10 Foundation report on the effect of TV violence on children
11 President leaving for a weekend vacation in the Bahamas
12 Preliminary plans for the 200th anniversary of the nation's independence in 1976

Ask another member of the class to evaluate you as a Gatekeeper. Survey members of your family to see whether they would have been interested in reading the stories you chose or whether they would have preferred other news on the list.

LAB PROFESSIONAL GATEKEEPERS

The aim of this lab is to compare front pages of different papers for the same date in order to find out how the professional Gatekeepers make their decisions.

Select one date, preferably one with a major news story, then consult the newspaper section of your library or write the Circulation Department of the papers listed below and ask for a copy of that day's paper. (Include 25 cents to cover the cost of the paper and postage.)

The <u>Atlanta</u> <u>Constitution</u> 10 Forsythe Street, Atlanta, Georgia 30302
The <u>Boston</u> <u>Record</u> <u>American</u> 5 Winthrop Square, Boston, Massachusetts 02106
The <u>Chicago</u> <u>Tribune</u> 435 North Michigan Avenue, Chicago, Illinois 60611
The <u>Christian</u> <u>Science</u> <u>Monitor</u> One Norway Street, Boston, Massachusetts 02115
The <u>Denver</u> <u>Post</u> 650 15th Street, Denver, Colorado 80202
The <u>Houston</u> <u>Chronicle</u> 512 Travis Street, Houston, Texas 77002
The <u>Indianapolis</u> <u>Star</u> 307 North Pennsylvania Street, Indianapolis, Indiana 46206
The <u>Louisville</u> <u>Courier-Journal</u> 525 West Broadway, Louisville, Kentucky 40202
The <u>Minneapolis</u> <u>Tribune</u> 5th and Portland, Minneapolis, Minnesota 55415
The <u>New</u> <u>York</u> <u>Times</u> Times Square, New York, New York 10036

When you have secured as many papers as you can for the same day, fill out the following:

Choice of Top Story (Banner headline, or top-of-page story)	Newspaper	Number of Editors who chose this story

Stories which appeared on the front page of all the papers you examined.

Stories which appeared on only one front page:

Newspaper:	Story:	Local Story?

FOCUS

How similar were the Gatekeepers'
choices of top stories?

Was there a pattern in their choices
that might be described as a "news
sense"?

How many of the choices might be ex-
plained by regional interests, the section
of the country which the paper serves?

On the basis of their choices, could any
of the newspapers be described as:

Sensational? (emphasis on crime, violence, scandal, popular newsmakers)

Politically partisan? (Democrat, Republican, other)

Regionally partisan? (local interests
dominate)

Wire service dominated? (few or no staff-
written stories)

> To seek the public's favor by presenting the news it wants
> to hear is to fail to understand the function of the press in
> a democracy. We are not in the business of winning pop-
> ularity contests. We are not in the entertainment business.
>
> WALTER CRONKITE

> Conflict is the bread and butter of TV news. It was when
> Negroes started getting hosed down in Birmingham and
> beaten on Freedom Rides and marches that television
> "discovered" the civil rights movement. When Watts and
> other urban ghettos exploded, television's viewers realized
> that the country outside of Dixie was sitting on a racial
> powder keg. And it was student uprisings, filmed by TV
> cameras, that brought the Nation face to face with the
> realities of Vietnam.
>
> RICHARD TOWNLEY

For the fact is that most of the individual news items in any newspaper—probably 75 to 85 per cent of them—never get broadcast at all. This is one of the very great strengths of the newspaper. . . . We are basically a headline service. . . . We transmit to a person a sample of events at the time they happened.   RICHARD GRAF

A typical metropolitan daily may receive approximately 8 million words of copy each day from its staff, wire services, feature syndicates, correspondents and special writers. Of this, only about 100,000 can be used in the paper.
DUANE BRADLEY

Because it is so dependent upon action, television runs the risk of being manipulated far more than the other news media.   JOHN GREGORY DUNNE

INTERFACE

Have you ever been responsible for preparing an agenda for a meeting? How did you exercise the power? Did you consult with others? Did you allow the initial plan to change as a result of what happened in the meeting? Did you think of yourself as a Gatekeeper?

Have you ever known anyone to exercise a Gatekeeper function on a family telephone?

INVESTIGATE

1   SELECT a story of sufficient importance that it is covered in several different news media, newspapers, news magazines, and possibly a TV magazine program. Note the difference in emphasis, factual detail, and "play" given to the same story in the different media.

2   Some of the most important decisions about coverage are made at a great distance from the news event itself. INTERVIEW some local editor about this fact.

3   ASK a newspaper or radio or television station if they will give you a bundle of wire service copy. Give the copy to different people and ask them to pick out their front page stories or their five-minute newscasts from the material. Compare their choices with the professional Gatekeepers'.

Few people expected any memorable remarks that night in Des Moines. It was another political fund-raising dinner, and Vice President Spiro Agnew was the featured speaker. But the Vice President proceeded to unleash what has become the classic query, or attack, on how the television network newsmen exercise their great gatekeeping power.

The night and its aftermath became memorable, indeed. Mr. Agnew followed this speech with several others in the same vein. News media of all kinds lashed back with cries of government intimidation and threats to freedom of the press. A great controversy ensued with charges and countercharges. Where would it end? Like all great issues, it was processed by the people, and it never really ends. The questions come up again and again.

In response to Mr. Agnew's question, "Now what do Americans know of the men who wield this power?" Time magazine printed brief biographies of the network executives and commentators. A major portion of the Agnew speech is reprinted here followed by the Time biographies.

The purpose of this lab is to focus on the Gatekeepers, raise the questions of who they are, and find out how they exercise their great power. The biographical information from Time will have to be updated, and a similar list should be drawn up identifying the Gatekeepers of your own local and regional media.

Television News Coverage

By Spiro T. Agnew, vice-president of the United States

. . . The purpose of my remarks tonight is to focus your attention on this little group of men who not only enjoy a right of instant rebuttal to every Presidential address, but, more importantly, wield a free hand in selecting, presenting and interpreting the great issues in our nation.

First, let's define that power. At least 40 million Americans every night, it's estimated, watch the network news. Seven million of them view A.B.C., the remainder being divided between N.B.C. and C.B.S.

According to Harris polls and other studies, for millions of Americans the networks are the sole source of national and world news. In Will Roger's observation, what you knew was what you read in the newspaper. Today for growing millions of Americans, it's what they see and hear on their television sets.

Now how is this network news determined? A small group of men, numbering perhaps no more than a dozen anchormen, commentators and executive producers, settle upon the 20 minutes or so of film and commentary that's to reach the public. This selection is made from the 90 to 180 minutes that may be available. Their powers of choice are broad.

They decide what 40 to 50 million Americans will learn of the day's events in the nation and in the world.

We cannot measure this power and influence by the traditional democratic standards, for these men can create national issues overnight.

They can make or break by their coverage and commentary a moratorium on the war.

They can elevate men from obscurity to national prominence within a week. They can reward some politicians with national exposure and ignore others.

For millions of Americans the network reporter who covers a continuing issue—like the ABM or civil rights—becomes, in effect, the presiding judge in a national trial by jury.

It must be recognized that the networks have made important contributions to the national knowledge—for news, documentaries and specials. They have often used their power constructively and creatively to awaken the public conscience to critical problems. The networks made hunger and black lung disease national issues overnight. The TV networks have done what no other medium could have done in terms of dramatizing the horrors of war. The networks have tackled our most difficult social problems with a directness and an immediacy that's the gift of their medium. They focus the nation's attention on its environmental abuses—on pollution in the Great Lakes and the threatened ecology of the Everglades.

But it was also the networks that elevated Stokely Carmichael and George Lincoln Rockwell from obscurity to national prominence.

Nor is their power confined to the substantive. A raised eyebrow, an inflection of the voice, a caustic remark dropped in the middle of a broadcast can raise doubts in a million minds about the veracity of a public official or the wisdom of a Government policy.

One Federal Communications Commissioner considers the powers of the networks equal to that of local state and Federal Governments all combined. Certainly it represents a concentration of power over American public opinion unknown in history.

Now what do Americans know of the men who wield this power? Of the men who produce and direct the network news, the nation knows practically nothing. Of the commentators, most Americans know little other than that they reflect an urbane and assured presence seemingly well-informed on every important matter.

We do know that to a man these commentators and producers live and work in the geographical and intellectual confines of Washington, D. C., or New York City, the latter of which James Reston terms the most unrepresentative community in the entire United States.

Both communities bask in their own provincialism, their own parochialism.

We can deduce that these men read the same newspapers. They draw their political and social views from the same sources. Worse, they talk constantly to one another, thereby providing artificial reinforcement to their shared viewpoints.

Do they allow their biases to influence the selection and presentation of the news? David Brinkley states objectivity is impossible to normal human behavior. Rather, he says, we should strive for fairness.

Another anchorman on a network news show contends, and I quote: "You can't expunge all your private convictions just because you sit in a seat like this and a camera starts to stare at you. I think your program has to reflect what your basic feelings are. I'll plead guilty to that."

Less than a week before the 1968 election, this same commentator charged that President Nixon's campaign commitments were no more durable than campaign balloons. He claimed that, were it not for the fear of hostile reaction, Richard Nixon would be giving into, and I quote him exactly, "his natural instinct to smash the enemy with a club or go after him with a meat axe."

Had this slander been made by one political candidate about another, it would have been dismissed by most commentators as a partisan attack. But this attack emanated from the privileged sanctuary of a network studio and therefore had the apparent dignity of an objective statement.

The American people would rightly not tolerate this concentration of power in Government.

Is it not fair and relevant to question its concentration in the hands of a tiny, enclosed fraternity of privileged men elected by no one and enjoying a monopoly sanctioned and licensed by Government?

The views of the majority of this fraternity do not—and I repeat, not—represent the views of America.

That is why such a great gulf existed between how the nation received the President's address and how the networks reviewed it. . . .

Our knowledge of the impact of network news on the national mind is far from complete, but some early returns are available. Again, we have enough information to raise serious questions about its effect on a democratic society. Several years ago Fred Friendly, one of the pioneers of network news, wrote that its missing ingredients were conviction, controversy and a point of view. The networks have compensated with a vengeance.

And in the networks' endless pursuit of controversy, we should ask: What is the end value—to enlighten or to profit? What is the end result—to inform or to confuse? How does the ongoing exploration for more action, more excitement, more drama serve our national search for internal peace and stability.

Gresham's Law seems to be operating in the network news. Bad news drives out good news. The irrational is more controversial than the rational. Concurrence can no longer compete with dissent.

One minute of Eldridge Cleaver is worth 10 minutes of Roy Wilkins. The labor crisis settled at the negotiating table is nothing compared to the confrontation that results in a strike—or better yet, violence along the picket lines.

Normality has become the nemesis of the network news. Now the upshot of all this controversy is that a narrow and distorted picture of America often emerges from the televised news.

A single, dramatic piece of the mosaic becomes in the minds of millions the entire picture. And the American who relies upon television for his news might conclude that the majority of American students are embittered radicals. That the majority of black Americans feel no regard for their country. That violence and lawlessness are the rule rather than the exception on the American campus.

We know that none of these conclusions is true.

Perhaps the place to start looking for a credibility gap is not in the offices of the Government in Washington but in the studios of the networks in New York.

Television may have destroyed the old stereotypes, but has it not created new ones in their places?

What has this passionate pursuit of controversy done to the politics of progress through local compromise essential to the functioning of a democratic society?

The members of Congress or the Senate who follow their principles and philosophy quietly in a spirit of compromise are unknown to many Americans, while the loudest and most extreme dissenters on every issue are known to every man in the street.

How many marches and demonstrations would we have if the marchers did not know that the ever-faithful TV cameras would be there to record their antics for the next news show?

We've heard demands that Senators and Congressmen and judges make known all their financial connections so that the public will know who and what influences their decisions and their votes. Strong arguments can be made for that view.

But when a single commentator or producer, night after night, determines for millions of people how much of each side of a great issue they are going to see and hear, should he not first disclose his personal views on the issue as well?

In this search for excitement and controversy, has more than equal time gone to the minority of Americans who specialize in attacking the United States—its institutions and its citizens? . . .

197

The "Unelected Elite"

Hundreds of men and women are responsible for the presentation of TV news, and any selection of an "elite" (in Spiro Agnew's phrase) is necessarily arbitrary. Still, a few men stand out at the top of the profession, including the twelve, some familiar and some not, who are identified below:

BRINKLEY, David, 49, NBC News correspondent. Born in Wilmington, N.C., dropped out of high school but took courses at University of North Carolina and Vanderbilt University. Reporter for Wilmington *Star-News*, 1938-41. Bureau manager in South for United Press Associations, 1941-43. Became NBC Washington correspondent, 1943; in 1956 was teamed with Huntley. Separated, three children.

CRONKITE, Walter, 53, managing editor of CBS News and news analyst. Born in St. Joseph, Mo., attended the University of Texas. War correspondent for United Press, 1942-45, and Chief U.P. correspondent at Nuremberg Trials; head of U.P. Moscow bureau, 1946-48. Correspondent CBS-TV news since 1950. Married, three children.

FRANK, Reuven, 48, president of NBC News. Born in Montreal, graduated from the City College of New York, 1942 (B.S.); Columbia, 1947 (M.S.). Reporter, Newark *Evening News*, 1947-49; night city editor, 1949-50. Joined NBC News in 1950; news editor, *Camel News Caravan*, 1951-54; producer, political convention coverage, 1956, 1960 and 1964; producer *Huntley-Brinkley Report*, 1956-62 and 1963-65. Married, two sons. Registered Democrat.

HUNTLEY, Chester (Chet), 57, NBC-News correspondent. Born in Cardwell, Mont., graduated from the University of Washington, 1934 (B.A.). Began radio newscasting with KPCB Seattle in 1934. Joined NBC in 1955, and within a year was teamed from New York with Brinkley in Washington. Married, two children. Registered as Independent.

LOWER, Elmer W., 56, president of ABC News. Born in Kansas City, Mo., graduated from University of Missouri School of Journalism, 1933; Columbia University, 1958 (M.A.). Reporter on the Louisville *Herald-Post* and Flint (Mich.) *Journal* and a United Press editor in Washington, D.C. Foreign correspondent, LIFE, 1944-51. CBS News, Washington and New York, 1953-59; vice president of NBC News, 1959-63. Married, two sons. Registered Independent.

MIDGLEY, Leslie, 54, CBS executive producer. Born in Salt Lake City, attended University of Utah. City editor, Salt Lake City *Deseret News*, 1935-40; night editor, New York *Herald-Tribune* Paris edition, 1944-49; associate editor, *Collier's*, 1949; managing editor, *Look*, 1952-54; producer, CBS News from 1954. Married (to Betty Furness), three children. Registered Democrat.

REYNOLDS, Frank, 45, ABC News analyst. Born in East Chicago, Ind., attended Indiana University and Wabash College. Anchor man at WBKB-TV, Chicago, 1950; writer-producer-reporter at WBBM-CBS, Chicago, 1951-63. ABC Chicago correspondent, 1963-65, and ABC White House correspondent, 1965-68. Married, five sons.

SALANT, Richard S., 55, president of CBS News. Born in New York City, graduated from Harvard, 1935 (A.B.) and Harvard Law School, 1938 (LL.B.). Attorney for U.S. Government, 1938-43, serving on National Labor Relations Board, with the Solicitor General and as acting director of the Attorney General's Committee on Administrative Procedure. Associate of law firm of Rosenman Goldmark, Colin & Kaye, 1946-48; partner, 1948-52. Vice president of CBS, 1952-61; named director of CBS and president of CBS News, 1961. Married, five children.

SEVAREID, (Arnold) Eric, 56, CBS News analyst. Born in Velva, N. Dak., graduated from University of Minnesota, 1935 (A.B.). Reporter on Minneapolis *Star*, 1936-37; city editor, Paris edition of the New York *Herald-Tribune*, 1938-39. Became CBS European correspondent, 1939; as U.S. war correspondent, broadcast French capitulation from Tours and Bordeaux; CBS Washington bureau, 1941-43 and 1946-59. Author of five books. Divorced, two children.

SMITH, Howard K., 55, ABC News analyst. Born in Ferriday, La., graduated from Tulane University, 1936 (B.A); Rhodes scholar at Oxford, 1937. Correspondent in London for United Press, 1939; CBS Berlin correspondent, 1941. War correspondent, 1944-45. Chief European correspondent of CBS in London, 1946-57. CBS Washington correspondent, 1957-61; CBS chief correspondent and general manager, 1961-62. Joined ABC in 1962. Author of three books. Married, two children.

WESTFELDT, Wallace, 46, executive producer of *Huntley-Brinkley*. Born in New Orleans, graduated from the University of the South, 1947 (B.A.). TIME correspondent, 1950 and 1952; reporter, Nashville *Tennessean*, 1953-61. Associate producer, NBC, 1961; writer for *Huntley-Brinkley*, 1963; associate producer in Washington, 1967. Married, one daughter.

WESTIN, Avram (Av) Robert, 40, ABC executive producer. Born in New York City, graduated from New York University, 1949 (B.A.); Columbia, 1958 (M.A.). CBS News writer-reporter, 1950-53; producer-director, 1958-67. Executive producer CBS News, 1965-67; executive director of Public Broadcasting Laboratory, 1967-69. Divorced, one son. An Independent.

Time
November 21, 1969

What responses would you give today to each of the questions Mr. Agnew raises? Specifically:

Who are the current network Gatekeepers?

Do you agree or disagree with Mr. Agnew when he says, "The views of the majority of this fraternity do not--and I repeat, not-- represent the views of America." Cite specific examples to support your position.

How much do the news broadcasts "reflect the basic feelings" of the network anchor-men?

Do you agree or disagree that the networks have a virtual monopoly on the TV news medium?

How do the different media separate the news from their news analysis? TV? Newspapers? Radio? News magazines? Is the distinction made clearly enough in each case?

Would you agree or disagree with Mr. Agnew that, "a narrow and distorted picture of America often emerges from the televised news." Cite specific instances to support your position.

INTERFACE

Do the editors or news directors in your school's news media represent a single group with a single viewpoint? If so, how does this influence their gatekeeping function?

Inquire who the Gatekeepers are in your local news media.

INVESTIGATE

1   MAKE a comparative analysis of news copy in a specific newspaper during an election period. Total up the column inches of space given to each competing candidate for one week prior to the election.

2   USE a periodical index and investigate the statements of the Gatekeepers in the "Selling of the Pentagon" controversy in July, 1971. Who made the decisions to produce and broadcast the program?

3   FIND OUT who made the decision to print "The Pentagon Papers" at the New York Times in June, 1971? At the Washington Post?

4   COMPILE a set of reactions by the press and the networks to Mr. Agnew's Des Moines speech. Are the arguments and evidence convincing?

5   VIEW the movie "Journalism: Mirror, Mirror on the World" and notice especially the role of the Gatekeeper. Was each Gatekeeper satisfied with his decisions after he had seen the coverage by other media?

One of the great concerns of privately owned and operated news media is the separation of the news from the opinions of the management. The positions and opinions of the owners are supposed to be restricted to editorial statements, and these statements are to be clearly identified as editorials.

Most of the information media in this country are privately owned. Some few are government subsidized. And some others function as the official organ of a special interest group like the English teachers or the United Auto Workers. These last publications are often non-profit operations owned by the membership and serving their own interests.

We in the audience need a fairly sophisticated set of tools to evaluate our information sources. Is this a disinterested news presentation or is it a special interest news release? The lab which follows offers a news release and a news report covering the same topic published at the same time.

 JET POLLUTION

The Fact Sheet printed below was distributed by the Air Transport Association of America. The news released in the Fact Sheet was also covered by Aviation Week & Space Technology, a weekly magazine published by McGraw-Hill. Both items appeared the last week in January, 1970.

Read both pieces, compare them, and answer the questions which follow.

AIR TRANSPORT ASSOCIATION OF AMERICA

FACT SHEET:

REDUCING POLLUTION FROM JET AIRCRAFT

JET EXHAUST EMISSIONS

Numerous studies have been made by air pollution control authorities, in cooperation with the airlines and engine manufacturers. These studies reveal that the principal emissions from jet exhaust are carbon monoxide, hydrocarbons, nitrogen oxides and particulates - mostly visible particles of unburned carbon that make up the smoke plume seen trailing jet engines. In every case, the amount contributed by aircraft is very small by comparison with all other sources of the same emission. In a December, 1968 report to the Congress, the Secretary of Health, Education and Welfare said aircraft emissions, as a percentage of total emissions from other sources, were: carbon monoxide - 1.2 percent; hydrocarbon - 0.7 percent; nitrogen oxide - 0.1 percent; particulate - 0.1 percent.

INDUSTRY PROGRAM

The relatively small proportion of total pollutants contributed by aircraft has not deterred the airlines and engine manufacturers from seeking ways to reduce objectionable jet aircraft exhaust emissions even further. The most objectionable of jet aircraft emissions - the smoke plume - has been the object of industry efforts for over ten years. Early progress was made as a by-product of the technological change from the first turbojet engines which used water injection on takeoff to the turbofan engine. More recent technological improvements have now brought significant progress, with the introduction of new almost smoke-free engines on new aircraft and the announcement of plans to begin retrofitting existing engines with smoke-reducing modifications.

SMOKE INCREASE HALTED

Engines on the new, wide-bodied jets (747, DC-10 and L-1011) are virtually smoke free. That is, their emissions are barely visible. (Anyone who has seen a 747 takeoff knows what this means.) These aircraft make up 85 percent of all new aircraft slated to be delivered to the airlines over the next four years. Thus, the increase of smoke from new aircraft entering the fleet has been stopped.

RETROFIT PROGRAM COMPLETE BY LATE 1972

A five-year old program to reduce the smoke from engines already in service has progressed to the point where the airlines on January 20 announced they would begin installing smoke reduction devices on JT8-D engines, and that the retrofit program would be substantially completed by 1972.

RETROFIT OF JT8-D WILL SOLVE MOST OF PROBLEM

The wisdom of the five-year old decision to start with the JT8-D is underscored by a study prepared last year for the National Air Pollution Control Administration by the Northern Research and Engineering Corporation. This study showed that the small jets powered by the JT8-D (Boeing 727, 737 and McDonnell-Douglas DC-9) contribute 55 percent of the smoke plume, based on daily landings and takeoffs. But when this figure is weighted by a factor to account for observed plume density, the JT8-D engine was found to contribute 70 percent of the jet aircraft smoke plume problem.

Some of the engines powering the long-range, four-engine jets also produce plumes as dense as the JT8-D, but their contribution to the total jet aircraft pollution problem is not so great because there are fewer of them and on the long-haul trips they make fewer landings and takeoffs per day.

WHAT DOES RETROFIT INVOLVE?

Reduced smoke combustors cannot be installed in an engine while it is still on the airplane. The engine must be taken off, moved into the engine overhaul shop and taken apart. The combustors and their associated components form part of what is called the "hot section" of the engine. Each JT8-D has nine combustors and associated components, such as fuel nozzles.

When all of the other parts of the hot section have been inspected and, where necessary, replaced or repaired, the engine must be reassembled. It is then run in a test cell to measure its performance at various power settings and insure that it is fit to be put on another airplane and go back into service.

-ATA-   1/20/70

U.S. Hands Airlines Anti-Smoke Timetable

Washington—Federal departments last week laid down an accelerated timetable for U.S. airlines to follow in installation of new combustors in Pratt & Whitney JT8D engines to reduce visible exhaust pollution.

Representatives of the carriers had expected to discuss the issue at a meeting with Health, Education and Welfare Secretary Robert H. Finch and Transportation Secretary John A. Volpe, but were told instead what the program was to be. Though some carriers were smarting over the political aspects, there were also those who considered the Federal program as practical and reasonable.

All 11 trunklines, nine local service carriers, six supplementals, Pan American World Airways, Pacific Southwest, Alaska, Seaboard World Airlines and Flying Tiger Line are to have the program "substantially completed" by the end of 1972.

The completion date represents a compromise between the program proposed by the Air Transport Assn., which called for completion by the end of 1974 (AW&ST Jan. 19, p. 25), and the earlier U.S. Health, Education and Welfare Dept. proposal, which called for almost immediate completion (AW&ST Sept. 22, 1969, p. 34).

After the meeting, Finch said the 1972 completion date will be conditional largely on the availability of the new burner cans from Pratt & Whitney. He said it is a "goal" rather than a "deadline."

Conversion kits are being produced at a rate of 45 per month now, and Finch said the rate is expected to increase to 200 per month by the end of the year. There will be about 3,000 engines involved. The JT8D is the only engine used on the McDonnell Douglas DC-9, Boeing 727 and 737.

Although Finch said the carriers were not pressured into the accelerated program, some airline spokesmen said they were presented with a "fait accompli" at the meeting. Another spokesman called it a masterful performance, while another said, "the whole thing was staged."

The airline representatives were invited to last week's meeting to discuss ways of reducing air pollution caused by jet aircraft emissions. But, significantly, the ATA, which has represented the airline industry throughout the smoke reduction program, was not invited. Consequently, some officials said they really did not have a spokesman during the meeting.

Before the meeting was announced, ATA President S. G. Tipton wrote to

John Shaffer, administrator of the Federal Aviation Administration, committing the airlines to a voluntary retrofit program to be completed by the end of 1974. The ATA's position on the retrofit program has been that there is not enough information on the new burner cans relating to durability and exhaust content, although it concedes they do reduce visible smoke emissions.

The most flight time on any retrofitted engine, according to the ATA, is about 3,000 hr. when at least 5,000 hr. is needed to establish reliability. Also, one airline maintains it is not known what is in the exhaust emission from a retrofitted engine, charging there is a possibility the harmful nitrogen oxide associated with jet engine exhaust might even be increased.

Despite this, Volpe said last week, "we have enough information to proceed." Under the announced agreement, however, the new burner cans will not be installed until engines are routinely brought in for overhaul, which will give airlines at least 5,000 hr. usage from the conventional burner cans.

Whether this agreement will become a common goal of the various states taking action against the airlines is yet to be seen. A significant one is New Jersey where trial date is set for Feb. 9 for the airlines to show why a temporary injunction should not be instituted to stop all traffic into Newark Airport using aircraft equipped with the JT8D engines.

New Jersey has called upon the airlines to begin installation of the burner cans immediately on all new jet aircraft and conversion of all existing engines by October, 1971.

The suit followed an investigation at Newark Airport last Apr. 11 and 28

and May 27. The State Health Dept. used the Ringelmann chart for determining pollution levels. The chart is a comparison scale used to estimate smoke opacity visually. The department concluded that the pollution found from the jet smoke was excessive by New Jersey standards, which are not necessarily the same as in other states.

The airlines believe that a federal regulation would pre-empt present and proposed state regulations and spare the airlines the possibility of different legal actions in each of the 50 states.

"The problem is national in scope and should be regulated by the Federal Aviation Administration and not the individual states," a spokesman for the airlines said. And Shaffer recently said the FAA is preparing to issue an advance notice of proposed rule making governing the emission of aircraft smoke while in flight.

But, former New Jersey Attorney General Arthur J. Sills said, "Environmental features are the subject matter of the health and welfare of the state and if we ask for something more than the federal agency we have the sovereignty to require compliance."

Sills said any settlement upon a timetable should be done in court to insure compliance without involving further law suits. "I'm not going to accept a compromise out of court. I want to see it in deed, under court order," he said.

The National Air Pollution Control Administration had tried to preclude a series of law suits by establishing a voluntary timetable for retrofitting last August. At that time the airlines refused and the Pollution Control Administration suggested legislation as the only alternative. . . .

Pratt & Whitney said it can meet the retrofitting requirements established with little lead time involved in orders. The company has received no orders, except for the cans used for testing by the airlines.

Pratt & Whitney also has proposed an alternative plan whereby the engine company would produce kits and the airlines would take existing cans and install modified burner elements.

How would you evaluate the Air Transport Association's Fact Sheet as a news source?

Do you think the Aviation Week & Space Technology article is an example of well researched and objective reporting?

Is there any evidence of bias, slanting, or "position-taking" in the AW & ST report? in the ATA Fact Sheet?

How would you evaluate the two items for comprehensiveness?

For the specialized knowledge of the reporter?

For the quality of the news sources?

 NEWS OF US

Contact someone in your community who publishes a newsletter for a non-profit organization such as the PTA, the Red Cross, the Community Fund, or a church group. Ask this editor/publisher to discuss the publication with the class. Be sure to have copies of the newsletter available in class.

Do the readers pay for the newsletter, is it included in a membership fee, or is it sent free of charge?

Does the editor assume the readers will expect and recognize a special interest slant in the newsletter?

Does the editor screen out information that is critical of the group? that threatens the interests of the group?

Make a list of other non-profit information media that you know of that have the same characteristics as the newsletter you examined above.

Considering the characteristics of the non-profit newsletter you examined, would you accept its information in the same way as you would information in a competitive, profit-making publication?

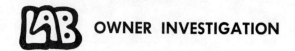 OWNER INVESTIGATION

Make a list of the news media and publications that members of the class most often come in contact with. Divide the class into task forces, and conduct an all-out investigation of the news media ownership.

Privately-owned, for profit media:

Who owns this news medium?

If the company is part of a publishing syndicate, what other news media do they produce?

Do they show diverse emphases?

Do they provide a voice for different audiences?

Do the owners have an editorial policy? a political preference?

If the medium claims to be politically independent, does it offer balanced news coverage at election time?

Is the medium part of a conglomerate made up of other businesses? Is it a profitable business enterprise? If not, why does the conglomerate keep it?

But a single company, in the nation's capital, holds control of the largest newspaper in Washington, D. C., and one of the four major television stations, and an all-news radio station, and one of the three major national news magazines—all grinding out the same editorial line. . . . For the purpose of clarity, before my thoughts are obliterated in the smoking typewriters of my friends in Washington and New York, let me emphasize I am not recommending the dismemberment of the Washington Post Company. I am merely pointing out that the public should be aware that these four powerful voices hearken to the same master.

SPIRO AGNEW

This is what makes the position of the broadcaster so difficult. Unlike the publisher, who brings in substantial sums from subscriptions and newsstand sales, the broadcaster has no second source of support. He is always serving two masters, advertiser and public. His service to his audience is restricted by what the advertisers will support.

WILLIAM RIVERS AND WILBUR SCHRAMM

Special-interest media:

How is the publication supported?

Who are the readers?

Is the special-interest character of the publication or medium clearly identifiable?

Is there a separation between ownership and editing responsibility?

Share the results of your ownership investigations by compiling a news media ownership catalog.

INTERFACE

How would you evaluate the objectivity of your school newspaper? Does its selection of news make it a special interest medium or a neutral news service providing the school with information needed for decision making?

Did anyone in the class investigate the ownership of the book companies which publish the textbooks used in your school? Do you think textbook publishers are influential media men? How do you think conglomerate business interests might affect the development of innovative textbooks?

Go through your daily newspaper and clip out any articles which show evidence of having originated with a special interest news release.

Are underground newspapers special interest or neutral? Be sure to base your evaluation on specific examples.

Make a listing of special interest information other than advertising that you have encountered in the past week.

INVESTIGATE

1 INVESTIGATE the growing number of newspaper companies that also own radio and television stations. What is the possibility of single-control news presentations in a community?

2 INVESTIGATE the emerging cable TV industry to find out whether ownership will be more diversified than the present major media, or will it be under much the same control.

3 COMPARE the British government owned-and-operated broadcasting network with the privately owned networks in the United States.

Where I Stand - Based on your experience with the units in this section, which of the following positions seems better to you?

a) The news process has become so complex today that it's impossible to say who's responsible for the finished product. It is not clear who to praise when it's good, or who to blame when it's bad.	b) The areas of influence in professional news reporting are still clear enough that people can evaluate the performance and assign responsibility for its strengths and weaknesses.

SIMULATE

Using the insights and conclusions you arrived at above, role play the following Media Man Simulation.

You are the producer of your network's weekend newscasts. You have been accused of over-emphasizing the sensational in news coverage in order to win viewers and advertisers away from the suddenly popular "happy news team" on a competing network. The chairman of the board has indicated that the advertising revenue must improve or the news budget will be cut.

This last week there was a nationwide protest against polluters, and you have good videotape from all over the country. The protest was generally peaceful. Only one affiliate station submitted pictures of a violent confrontation. But this one confrontation between students and plant security guards ended with three persons hospitalized, one in critical condition. Will you run this footage? How will you keep a balanced picture of non-violence, or will you try?

the mass media
in a democratic society

The first two parts of this inquiry program have attempted to explore the dynamic processes which determine what we see and hear and experience in the mass media.

This third part goes one step further and asks, what can we do to influence and change the media. Theorists point out that the mass media are by far the most pervasive and persuasive force forming popular taste, public attitudes, and political opinion in our society. Government regulates and influences the media; but government has its own interests as well. The healthy tension which should exist between the media, the government, and the public is often lacking because one part of the triangle, the public, doesn't use its power. The public doesn't speak up.

What is the people's right to know? How can we, the public, talk back to the mass media? These questions are at the heart of media ecology. What can we do to influence and improve the media environment which we live in and which is so critical to the quality of life in our democratic society?

The freedom of the press is one of the bulwarks of liberty, and can never be restrained but by despotic governments.

VIRGINIA BILL OF RIGHTS

Congress shall make no law respecting an establishment of religion, or prohibiting the free exercise thereof; or abridging the freedom of speech, or of the press; or the right of the people peaceably to assemble, and to petition the government for redress of grievances.

FIRST AMENDMENT, U. S. CONSTITUTION

The theory of a free press is that the truth will emerge from free reporting and free discussion, not that it will be presented perfectly and instantly in any one account. . . . A free press is not a privilege but an organic necessity in a great society.

WALTER LIPPMANN

If it happened, the people are entitled to know. There is no condition that can be imposed on that dictum without placing between the people and the truth a barrier of censorship— . . .

WALTER CRONKITE

The People's Right to Know

The right to know, to receive information we need to organize our lives and to participate in our government, is a social right, a direct right which belongs to every person in a democratic society. We cannot exercise our public responsibilities if we are not adequately informed. We cannot respond to something we don't know about.

And yet there are certain matters which by their very nature seem to call for classification or control of information. Patrick Henry set out the terms of this perennial debate. The government, he said, must keep from the press "such transactions as relate to military operations or affairs of great consequence, the immediate promulgation of which might defeat the interests of the community." On the other hand, the press must prevent officials from "covering with the veil of secrecy the common routine of business; for the liberties of the people never were, or never will be, secure when the transactions of their rulers may be concealed from them."

The debate goes on. The probes which follow are intended to give you a first-hand experience with the challenge of understanding, interpreting, and safeguarding the people's right to know.

PROBE

How does classification of information affect the people's right to know?

It is easy to confuse classification of information with censorship. They are similar, and society must deal with both of them. When information is classified, those who know impose secrecy on themselves and the facts because they believe the community would be harmed if the facts were known. With censorship, someone else, someone in authority, imposes the restriction of information on another.

Notice the difference. If a combat soldier writing home decides not to reveal military information which would harm the war effort, he restricts the information himself, and in effect "classifies" it. But if the combat soldier divulges important military information in his letter and a military censor removes it before the letter reaches his family--that is censorship.

The power to classify information is a delicate, two-edged power. It can be used to protect the community or the nation, but it can also be used to conceal from the people what they have a right to know. The purpose of this lab is to provide you with an experience of the problems involved in classifying information.

 **RELEASE OR CLASSIFY?**

Each of the situations described below involves a group of people with the power to classify information. Have the class divide into groups according to their interests in the proposed situations, discuss the problems, and decide in each case whether to release or classify the information.

When the deliberations are complete, share the results. What was decided in each case and why?

Situation A: House Education Committee

You are state representatives, members of the House Education Committee which is permitted to hold closed meetings. In one of these closed meetings you have considered the rising costs of your state colleges and universities. The majority of the committee favors a bill to raise tuition by one-third. In earlier open hearings representatives of community-operated junior colleges opposed these tuition hikes on the grounds that more students would then enter their junior colleges and the local communities would wind up paying for the state's decision. The junior college people threatened a powerful lobby against the bill if it came to the floor of the legislature. You have now appointed three members of your committee to draft the tuition hike bill. It will take several weeks to complete. Will you release your committee decision to the news media? If so, when?

Situation B: Board of Health

You are doctors, members of the County Health Board, called together for an emergency meeting on mercury poisoning. Within the past three days five cases of mercury poisoning have been reported by different hospitals in the county. None of the attending physicians has been able to trace the cause, but two of the victims had definitely eaten fish within two days of their attacks. Water specimens are now being tested and sample fish from nearby lakes and rivers are being checked for mercury content. The county government has been under fire for failing to enforce adequate pollution controls. Should you, the County Health Board, notify the news media about the number of poisonings at this time, before all the evidence is in?

Situation C: Police Review Board

You are members of your local police review board. Up until now it had been the policy for the police to withhold the names of persons under sixteen years of age who have been arrested. In the past three weeks there has been a series of fights after the high school basketball games. The situation is reaching crisis proportions. The police can count on a fight with personal and property damage after every game. Some coaches have pointed out that athletes who violate rules are thrown out of the game and always mentioned in sports reports. So why not change the police policy and release the names of the juveniles who start these fights? Will you change the policy and release these names to the news media or not?

Situation D: Union Bargaining Team

You are the bargaining team for the city transportation workers union. You have threatened a strike which will shut down all the bus service in the city. After ten hours of deliberation you feel you are about to come to an acceptable compromise with the city on your contract requests. But you still have no official word from the city; the settlement terms have come through rumors from reliable sources. The strike is announced for midnight tonight. The people are concerned about how they will get to work tomorrow. It seems a hard line is necessary to be sure the city will come to terms before midnight, but the people want information now. What will you say to the news media?

Situation E: Presidential Advisers

You are special advisers to the president of the United States. An official of the State Department has defected and taken up residence in a Latin American country. The defection is bound to create international comment, but other governments are not aware of the high level strategy meetings the man participated in or the personal differences he had with the Secretary of State. Should the information of his defection be released from Washington or come from international capitols? If from Washington, how much information about the official should be released? Should a statement from the Secretary of State be issued?

Situation F: Campaign Staff

You are close friends and political advisers of George Williams who is beginning his campaign for governor of your state. George had an unfortunate experience as a college student; explainable, but not likely to be acceptable to many voters. He was involved in a dormitory fire which killed his roommate. A group of students gathered together in a small room, there was some horseplay with fireworks, a challenge, a flash fire, and George panicked and ran. The circumstances were never made public. The college never revealed the cause of the fire. The coroner's report was classified. Will you advise George to tell the whole story or will you risk the opponent's suggestions about what happened?

Situation G: School Records Committee

You are members of a special committee called to review the school records policy. Many requests are made for information from student's records--grades, conduct, attendance records, character analysis. Just recently a local news reporter called for this kind of information about an alumnus arrested in a protest demonstration. What is your opinion? What information, if any, should be revealed? How will you formulate the records policy?

Record the decision to release or classify the information of each of the groups. Note the reasons.

A House Education Committee   Why?

B Board of Health   Why?

C Police Board   Why?

D Union Team   Why?

E Presidential Advisers   Why?

F Campaign Staff   Why?

G School Records Committee   Why?

Using these situations as the basis for your conclusions, can you say whether the decision to classify information is generally motivated by concern for society in general or for private and special interests?

How much of a factor in the groups' decisions was the awareness that any information they wished to classify would probably reach the public sooner or later and the news media would then inquire why the information was withheld?

Is the danger of sensational or unbalanced coverage by the news media a good reason to classify information?

What recorded information about yourself would you like to have classified or kept classified?

What school information is not available to the student press? Faculty meetings? Administration committee meetings? Standardized test results for the school? Student records? Do you think the classification of this information is warranted?

How many decision-making groups in your community hold closed meetings? Do the news media report these meetings anyway? If so, how? How do you rate the credibility of these stories?

INVESTIGATE

1 FIND OUT what documents in your city and county files are kept classified. Wills? Birth records? Real estate assessments?

2 SELECT a major historic situation in which information was concealed from the public and trace the consequences. Examples: President Woodrow Wilson's health; splitting of the atom and making of the first atom bombs; Yalta talks and agreements ending World War II; the Pentagon Papers.

3 INTERVIEW a local reporter to find out what information needed by the public in the community is most difficult to obtain.

Censorship is a restriction or suppression of information by someone in authority who judges the information objectionable for moral, political, military, or other reasons. The exercise of censorship has always been controversial. From the earliest history of man people in power and authority have acted as censors. Pharoahs controlled publications in Egypt. Puritans legislated moral regulations. Parents always place some books, shows, and movies "off limits" for their children. Many governments and dictators today keep strict control of their information media. Even in democratic societies which depend upon the free flow of information there are attempts made by government or by special interest groups to limit the freedom of the press. United States history has seen the Alien and Sedition Acts which suppressed publishers critical of public officials, the suppression of the Copperhead Press sympathetic to the Confederacy, the McCarthy senate committee which blacklisted writers, broadcasters, and filmmakers, and the injunction against publication of the Pentagon Papers.

The purpose of the lab which follows is to give you an experience of the dynamics and difficulties of censorship, to help you form your own judgment about this controversial issue.

LAB PRINT POLICY

Divide the class into groups of about six persons each; ask one adult to join each group if possible. Each group will consider itself the school's newly appointed committee to establish a policy statement for school publications. The policy statement should cite any type of printed material that is unacceptable for publication, and it should also outline what action should be taken in the event that such unacceptable material does appear in a school publication.

Perhaps some of the committees will feel the need for information on recent court decisions concerning freedom of the press as it applies to school publications. A select bibliography on the topic appears in the Mass Media Guide, but the courts are constantly modifying their interpretation of the law and you may want to consult a lawyer or someone in the school district office who is informed on the latest interpretations of the law.

When the policy statements are formulated, duplicate them so that everyone can discuss the similarities and differences in each.

Print Policy Statement:

Do the policy statements allow for a free
flow of information? opinion? controversy?
expression?

If there are major differences in ideas and
values in the various policy statements,
list them below.

 APPLYING THE POLICY

Choose one of the policy statements from those submitted above. It becomes the law.
The class should then select one of its members to be a policy interpreter. Ask the
school principal to select another policy interpreter, someone he would trust. Ask a
publications adviser to select a third policy interpreter.

Those who have been chosen to interpret the publication policy are now ready to make
some decisions. The Mass Media Guide contains reprints of several articles which
have appeared in school publications. Assume that these articles have just been published in one of your school's publications, subject to the new guidelines. Other materials may also be submitted.

Each policy interpreter should read the copy submitted and judge it according to the
publication policy statement. Decisions may be written or reported to the class together with the reasons for each decision.

Compare the decisions of the policy interpreters. If they were similar, how were
they consistent?

If they were dissimilar, indicate which
interpreters interpreted the policy more
strictly or more loosely on the chart
below.

If the policy interpreters were censors
and had the power to prohibit publication,
would any of the materials submitted have
failed to reach the public?

Would you agree with the restraint orders,
if there were any? Would you have restrained anything the censors permitted?

From this simulation, who would you say
is more influential in the censorship process,
the policy makers or the interpreters of the
policy?

Based on this simulation, what does the class
think about media censorship?

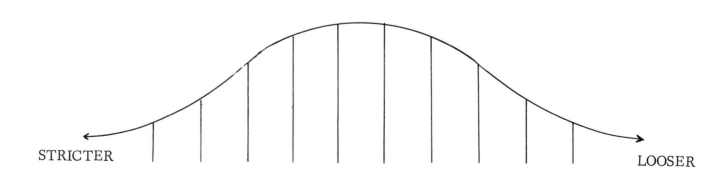

STRICTER   LOOSER

INTERFACE

What policy do you think should exist in your family with regard to receiving mail or phone calls?

Are the "X" and "R" movie ratings effective? Are they enforced by local theater management? Do you think the motion picture industry does a good job of self-regulation?

Have any groups in your community boycotted stores that they charged were selling indecent literature? What is your attitude toward this type of boycott?

What is your attitude toward the underground press, toward controversial publications and films that offend many persons in the community? Should these media enjoy the full freedom of the press? What issues are at stake here?

Do you think there are any situations in which censorship activity is called for?

INVESTIGATE

1 FIND OUT what laws may be on the books in your community to control the content and distribution of print and film media.

2 INVESTIGATE the history of the Hays Office of the Motion Picture Producers and Distributors of America, established in 1922.

3 INVESTIGATE the blacklisting of authors, directors, and film producers called before the McCarthy Senate Committee in the early 1950's.

4 INTERVIEW a knowledgeable lawyer or research cases involving the First Amendment guarantee of free press. Specifically:

The Alien and Sedition Acts (1812)

The problems of the Copperhead Press during the Civil War

The Minnesota Gag Law Case (283 U.S. 697, 1931)

The Postmaster General Hennigan vs. Esquire magazine case

The Roth vs. United States case (354 U.S. 476, 1957)

The controversy and congressional action following the 1971 CBS-TV documentary "The Selling of the Pentagon."

The legal action surrounding the publishing of the Pentagon Papers in the New York Times, 1971

5 EXAMINE how economic censorship can be a powerful force to restrict freedom of the press. A revealing case involved a Michigan newspaper; look up the story in Time, December 28, 1970, page 23.

Where I Stand - Based on your experience with the units in this section, which of the following positions seems better to you?	
a) A government must limit the freedom of its citizens to the extent that it must guard all the people against the irresponsible use of freedom by some. Therefore, even the officials of a democracy must have the power to censor the media and to classify information.	b) Government officials who have the power to censor or to classify information are human and can make mistakes. They are likely to use this power for their own interests rather than for the public interest. They may use it to keep themselves in office. Therefore public officials should be given almost no power to censor the media or to classify information.

SIMULATE Using the insights and conclusions you arrived at above, role play the following Media Man Simulation.

You are the president of a large state university. The school newspaper is staffed by student radicals. It promotes protests, supports minority groups on all issues, and gives scarcely any coverage to athletics, social events, or other traditional campus activities. Some columnists use language offensive to some readers, especially some members of your board of trustees.

You have made a survey which indicates that most students do not read the newspaper. Some have petitioned that the paper be discontinued or its contents controlled. You have received many letters from people in the community asking you to take action against the paper. The board of trustees has indicated you should do something about it. And state legislators, who control funds, have threatened an investigation.

But the staff of the paper was selected by established procedures and they have made it clear that any action on your part would be a violation of freedom of the press. What will you do?

Broadcast stations are licensed to serve the "public convenience, interest, or necessity." . . . Licensees are expected to ascertain and meet the needs of their communities in programming. Applicants must show how community needs and interests have been determined and how they will be met. The Commission periodically reviews station performance, usually in connection with the license renewal application, to determine whether the licensee has lived up to its obligations and the promise it made in obtaining permission to use the public airwaves.

FEDERAL COMMUNICATIONS COMMISSION

The press release—The most widely used tool in publicity work. When you want something in the papers, you write it out in the form of a news story and send it to the editors. Every edition of every newspaper contains news that originated in this way.

RICHARD FRISBIE

Feedback and Feed-in

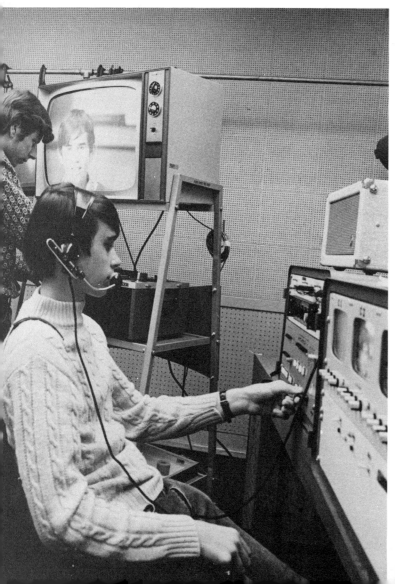

The people have a right to know. But we, the people, also have a responsibility to talk back to the media, to express our feelings and judgments, to take an active part in influencing and improving our media environment.

What can we do? This lab will be open-ended, a few suggestions and proposals on how you can feed back your reactions to your mass media sources.

LAB LETTERS

It is an easily documented fact that in relation to the mass audiences they serve the television networks receive almost no mail in reaction to their programming, treatment of news, or advertising policies. View at least two episodes of a series show or watch a TV special report, discuss your reactions with others, and write a letter of comment, positive or negative, to the network.

Continuity Acceptance Department
ABC Television Network
1330 Avenue of the Americas
New York, New York 10019

Program Practices Division
CBS Television Network
51 West 52nd Street
New York, New York 10019

Program Standards and Practices
NBC Television Network
30 Rockefeller Plaza
New York, New York 10020

For further information regarding a specific network, agency, or group related to broadcasting, contact the following:

Industry Associations

National Association of Broadcasters
1661 N Street, NW
Washington, D. C. 20036

Television Information Office
745 Fifth Avenue
New York, New York 10022

Citizens Organizations

Action for Children's Television
33 Hancock Avenue
Newton Centre, Massachusetts 01259

Action on Smoking and Health
2000 H Street, N.W.
Washington, D.C. 20006

American Council for Better
  Broadcasts with TACT
17 West Main
Madison, Wisconsin 53703

Anti-Defamation League
1640 Rhode Island Avenue, N.W.
Washington, D.C. 20036

Citizens Communications Center
1816 Jefferson Place, N.W.
Washington, D.C. 20036

Institute for American
  Democracy, Inc.
1330 Massachusetts Avenue, N.W.
Washington, D.C. 20005

Institute for Policy Studies
1520 New Hampshire Avenue, N.W.
Washington, D.C. 20036

National Association for Better
  Broadcasting
373 Northwestern Avenue
Los Angeles, California 90004

National Audience Board, Inc.
152 East End Avenue
New York, New York 10028

National Citizens Committee for
  Broadcasting
609 Fifth Avenue
New York, New York 10017

Office of Communication
United Church of Christ
289 Park Avenue South
New York, New York 10010

Television, Radio & Film Commission
The Methodist Church
475 Riverside Drive
New York, New York 10027

The Federal Government

Federal Communications Commission
1919 M Street, N.W.
Washington, D.C. 20554

LAB   LICENSES

"You ought to know that every three years all the radio and television station licenses come up for renewal in your state. You
ought to know when that date is. It is an 'election day' of sorts,
and you have a right and obligation to 'vote.' Not surprisingly,
many individuals have never even been told there's an election.

". . . Congress has provided that the airwaves are public property.
The user must be licensed, and, in the case of commercial broadcasters, that license term is for three years. There is no 'right'
to have the license renewed. It is renewed only if past performance,
and promises of future performance, are found by the FCC to serve
'the public interest.' In making this finding, the views of local individuals and groups are, of course, given great weight. In extreme cases, license revocation or license renewal contest proceedings may be instituted by local groups."

Nicholas Johnson, Commissioner
Federal Communication Commission

Check the accompanying table and see when the licenses for the radio and television stations in your state are up for renewal. If the time is right, write the FCC
to compliment or criticize one or other of your local stations. Are they actually
serving the public interest? Are they responsive to the needs of your local community in broadcasting news, public affairs, local talent and entertainment?

All licenses within a given state expire on the same date. Stations must file for license renewal with the FCC ninety days prior to the expiration date. Petitions to deny a station's license renewal application must be filed between ninety and thirty days prior to the expiration date. Forthcoming expiration dates (subject to change) for stations located in the following states include:

Florida, Puerto Rico, and the Virgin Islands: February 1, 1973; 1976; and 1979.

Alabama and Georgia: April 1, 1973; 1976; and 1979.

Arkansas, Louisiana, and Mississippi: June 1, 1973; 1976; and 1979.

Tennessee, Kentucky, and Indiana: August 1, 1973; 1976; and 1979.

Ohio and Michigan: October 1, 1973; 1976; and 1979.

Illinois and Wisconsin: December 1, 1973; 1976; and 1979.

Iowa and Missouri: February 1, 1974; 1977; and 1980.

Minnesota, North Dakota, South Dakota, Montana, and Colorado: April 1, 1974; 1977; and 1980.

Kansas, Oklahoma, and Nebraska: June 1, 1974; 1977; and 1980.

Texas: August 1, 1974; 1977; and 1980.

Wyoming, Nevada, Arizona, Utah, New Mexico, and Idaho: October 1, 1974; 1977; and 1980.

California: December 1, 1974; 1977; and 1980.

Washington, Oregon, Alaska, Guam, and Hawaii: February 1, 1975; 1978; and 1981.

Connecticut, Maine, Massachusetts, New Hampshire, Rhode Island, and Vermont: April 1, 1975; 1978; and 1981.

New Jersey and New York: June 1, 1975; 1978; and 1981.

Delaware and Pennsylvania: August 1, 1975; 1978; and 1981.

Maryland, the District of Columbia, Virginia, and West Virginia: October 1, 1972, 1975, 1978, and 1981.

North Carolina and South Carolina: December 1, 1972; 1975; 1978; and 1981.

"You have only to exercise your imagination to improve the programing service of your local station. Student groups, civic luncheon clubs, unions, PTAs, the League of Women Voters, and so forth are in an ideal position to accomplish change. They can contact national organizations, write for literature, and generally inform themselves of their broadcasting rights. Members can monitor what is now broadcast and draw up statements of programing standards, indicating what they would like to see with as much specificity as possible. They can set up Citizens Television Advisory Councils to issue reports on broadcasters' performance. They can send delegations to visit with local managers and owners. They can, when negotiation fails, take whatever legal steps are necessary with the FCC. They can complain to sponsors, networks, and local television stations when they find commercials excessively loud or obnoxious."

Nicholas Johnson, Commissioner
Federal Communication Commission

The name of the game is media access, effective use of the media to make your voice heard, to represent your views on a current issue. The availability of the media makes the difference in capturing interest and molding public opinion.

Media access is not just for professionals. Community organizations, common cause, minority groups, and students all make use of the media to support their causes and to publicize their needs. A battered mimeograph machine or a cassette recorder are enough to do the job.

This probe challenges you to take the insights and conclusions you have stored up during your trip through Mass Media and explode them in creative media production.

 MEDIA ACCESS

The first task is to find some group that would benefit from access to the media and publicity for its cause. Look around your community. Are there struggling social action groups that could use media assistance? Is there an environmental group? Are there migrant workers or hospital patients, or wards of the court, or other people in need of justice who would be helped by public exposure of their needs? Is there a community organization with a minimal budget which could use your assistance? Look around your school. What are the non-publicized activities? What issues or groups could be helped by publicity?

The class should spend some time brainstorming the various issues, groups, and approaches for this media access project. As the issues and groups emerge, the class should divide into interest groups and further brainstorm the best ways to publicize the problems they have identified.

Now look at the following "mediography" to find out how other groups have used the media in simple yet creative ways to give public exposure to important issues.

Television

WJA-TV is a student-centered television project sponsored by WNDU-TV, Notre Dame University's NBC affiliate in South Bend, Indiana. The project is designed for high school sophomores, juniors, and seniors and offers a first-hand encounter with all of the responsibilities faced by commercial broad-casters. Managerial problems, production techniques, creative writing and performing, and commercial advertising sales are all part of the "curriculum" of the project, now in its eleventh year of operation.

"The Carlmont Hour" Last year Carlmont High School became one of the first schools in California to produce programs for regular weekly transmission over community cable television. Events of campus and community interest are recorded each week on video tape and cablecast by the Peninsula Cable Television Company. The programs are shown from 6 to 7 p.m. each Thursday for viewing by a potential audience of more than 10,000 CATV subscribers.

"Newsseekers" is a public affairs news show broadcasting weekly on KCET, Channel 28, an educational TV station in Los Angeles. The entire show is written, filmed, edited, produced, and performed by the students at Pacoima Junior High School, Pacoima, California.

"Treehouse" is a teen talk show featuring a pair of 13-year-old youngsters and an all-teen orchestra aired over UHF Channel 39, KTVT-TV, Dallas.

All of the above programs are described at length in the Winter, 1972 issue of Communication: Journalism Education Today.

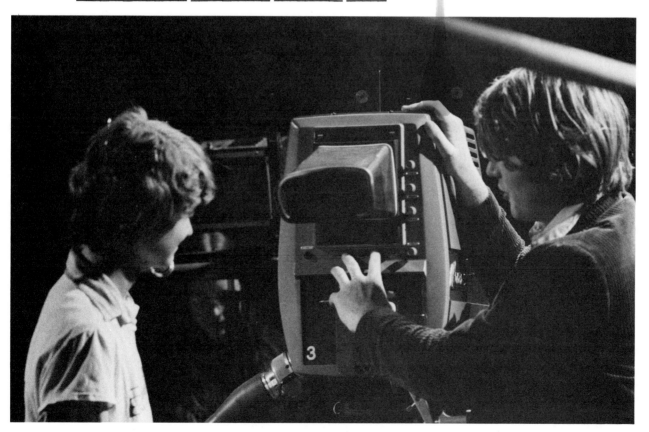

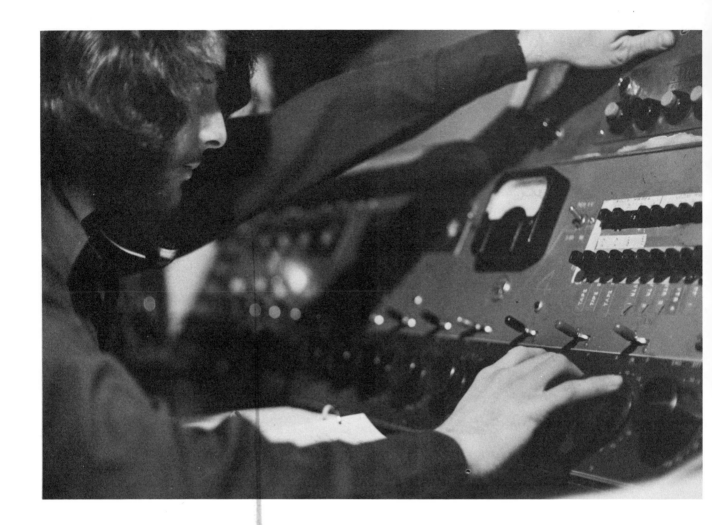

Radio

There are over one hundred high school FM stations in the country. The format of each station is different but it generally includes live coverage of school sports and musical events, student-announced news and weather, comment on current issues, plus a varied music program played by student disk jockeys.

Look under Educational FM Stations in the current Broadcasting Yearbook in your library to find the school station nearest you. Contact them to find out what they broadcast and how they do it. You might make and send them taped programs for broadcast.

Print

The A.B. Dick Company offers a MEDIA ACCESS KIT with information on the availability and use of offset printing equipment, how to estimate print costs, and "how we did it" articles from students who have developed media access projects. Write MEDIA ACCESS KIT, A. B. Dick Company, 5700 Touhy Avenue, Niles, Illinois 60648. Enclose 25 cents for postage and handling.

Film

Six high school seniors created a furor in Passaic, New Jersey with an eleven-minute film titled "Passaic is a River City." This 8mm documentary focused on aspects of the city that needed improvement: air and water pollution, factory wastes, lack of entertainment facilities, and the apathy of the people. After some emotional reaction by the city council, the film stimulated many civic improvements.

A Super-8 film made by students for a biology class in Atlanta helped save parkland about to be sold for condominum housing.

A carefully planned, well shot, honestly edited film may give the best media access to a cause or issue you wish to promote.

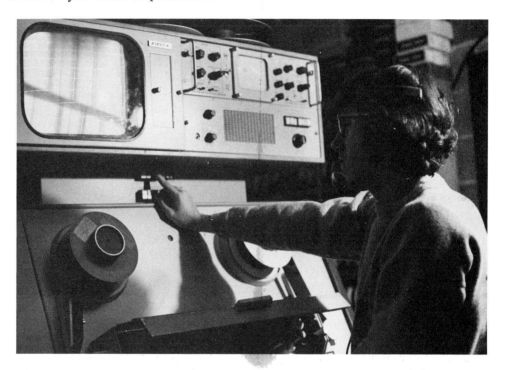

Videotape

Eighteen-year-olds in several major cities have been urged to register to vote by student-made videotapes. The tapes explain registration and voting procedures. They were played in parks, on beaches, on campuses, and in other places where students gather.

Young people in Milwaukee effectively used half-inch videotape to carry a minority candidate's message to the people in a recent mayoral election. He couldn't afford regular TV commercial costs and air time rates.

A student-made videotape on threatened cutbacks in art, music, and gym classes in Chicago's public schools helped convince parents to organize and express their views.

Simple videotape equipment can be carried anywhere and played for anyone. Try it yourself.

Your challenge is to define precisely how best to use the media to provide maximum exposure to the problem area or issue you have chosen. Perhaps flyers, posters, handbills, a light show, a radio program, a photo essay. Perhaps an article with pictures for a newspaper or magazine, a film or a slide-sound show. Perhaps a wall newspaper, phone calls to a radio talk show. Perhaps media combinations will give your issue the best exposure.

Before, during, and after your work with the people or cause you choose to promote, make the following assessments:

1 Are you sure you are furnishing publicity assistance to people who actually want it, that you are not intruding?

2 Make an economic assessment of your project and carefully budget available funds. How will your media program be funded?

3 Make a time assessment. If you are going to work with a group of people, you should get sufficiently involved in their circumstances to represent them accurately to the public.

4 Make a resources assessment. What people, talents, equipment do you need to do your task effectively?

5 Finally, evaluate the finished project. Was it effective? How could it have been more effective? What were its weak points? Did you make the most efficient use of the media you had available to you?

Where I Stand -

Based on your experience with the units in this section, which of the following positions seems better to you?

a) Today's mass media offer a record and reflection of our society's life and times that is both informational and entertaining. Accordingly, we can take it or leave it, but we need not feel any responsibility for this media output.

b) As media consumers we share a responsibility for the accuracy and faithfulness of the image which the media project of the life and times in our society. This responsibility demands our involvement in the media processes. Our critical input counts.

SIMULATE

Using the insights and conclusions you arrived at above, role play the following Media Man Simulation.

You are planning a utopia, an ideal future society with perfect government, communications, and social conditions. Using the data and ideas you have come up with in this course, project yourself into the future. Dream and create an ideal society in which the mass media will involve and serve and totally liberate its citizens. Project beyond computers and picturephones to lasers and wrap-around portable television.

Here are some points to consider: Will our current mass media be around? What new media? Who will own and operate the "newspaper"? What form will it take? Will there be advertising? What will the role of the reporter be? Will there be censorship? Classified information? Will the government license and control the media? With the possibility of direct communication through the emotions, how will I accommodate my positions with yours?

Brainstorm and discuss these issues in class. Develop a media plan for your society. Name the new utopia. Give a verbal-visual demonstration of how it will work and how media will serve the people.

ACKNOWLEDGMENTS

With the other books in the ComEd Series, Persuasion and Exploring Television, Mass Media is published to help realize the goals of the Curriculum Commission of the Journalism Education Association. From 1965 to 1969 the active members of that commission conceived the ideas for curriculum reform that are incorporated in this book.

A. C. Nielsen Company, for furnishing the booklets "What the Ratings Really Mean" and "Nielsen Television."

AP Newsfeatures, for permission to reproduce the Canadian air crash broadcast wire reports.

Aviation Week & Space Technology, for permission to reprint "U. S. Hands Airlines Anti-Smoke Timetable."

Chicago Daily News, for permission to reprint "Inside the Conspiracy 7 Trial" by Raymond R. Coffey, "Prison Rebels ask 'human' treatment" by John Linstead, and "Malcolm X College's new look" by Betty Washington.

Chicago Tribune, "Men of Mercy? Profit in Pain" by William Jones; "I Was a White Student at Malcolm X" by Fredric Soll; and an excerpt from "Who Got Zonkers Off the Ground" by Les Bridges. All articles reprinted, courtesy of the Chicago Tribune.

Los Angeles Times Syndicate, for "TV Techniques Raise Questions" by Flora Lewis. Copyright, 1971, Newsday. Reprinted with permission.

Mad Magazine, for permission to reprint the "Do-It-Yourself Protest Newspaper Story" © 1968 by E. C. Publications, Inc.

New York Times, "The Shelling of the Pentagon" by Robert Sherrill © 1971 by The New York Times Company. Reprinted by permission.

Newsweek Magazine, for permission to reprint "The Selling of Congress," Copyright Newsweek, Inc., 1971.

Reuters Limited, for permission to reprint "Air Crash Killing 108 probed."

Saturday Review and Nicholas Johnson, Commissioner, Federal Communications Commission, for permission to reprint excerpts from "What Do We Do About Television." Copyright 1970 Saturday Review, Inc.

Standard Rate & Data Service, Inc., for permission to reprint Publishers' Editorial Profiles from Consumer Magazine Rates & Data for June 1972. Also for permission to reprint "In The Seventies . . . You've Got a Lot to Live" by James B. Somerall from Mediascope Magazine for April 1970.

Time Magazine, "The Unelected Elite" and "Death At the Hospital." Reprinted by permission from Time, The Weekly Newsmagazine; © Time, Inc., 1969, 1970.

Illustration

John Druska, cover and title page; Ken Bobowski, 240; William Bollin, 20 (top), 31 (right), 55, 223 (top right); Courtesy of CBS Television, 173, 177, 180, 186; Courtesy of the Chicago Daily News, 133; Courtesy of the Chicago Tribune, 139, 140, 141, 145, 146, 180 (top), 199; William Crowley, C.S.Sp., 31 (left), 43, 113, 157, 231 (bottom), 236 (left); Donald Doll, S.J., 27, 32, 69, 88 (top), 94, 178, 193, 204, 217, 221, 223 (lower right), 232, 238; John Glaser, 85 (right); Algimantas Kezys, S.J., 7-10; Robert Kunstmann, 20 (bottom), 27 (lower right), 34, 56 (top), 97, 108 (top), 117, 120 (top), 126, 136, 137, 150, 169, 185, 190, 208, 218, 223 (left), 226 (top), 231 (right); NASA, 111; Courtesy of NBC Television, 85 (left), 158, 212 (top); St. Ignatius College Prep, Chicago, 24 (right), 33 (left), 87, 149, 179, 225; Dick Sangal, Courtesy of Communication: Journalism Education Today, 226 (lower left); Sam Schwartz, 33 (right); Courtesy of the Seeburg Corporation, 38, 40; Tom Stack, 236 (right); James Strzok, S.J., 24 (left); James Vorwoldt, S.J., 44, 56 (bottom), 88 (bottom), 95, 108 (bottom), 120 (bottom), 172, 180, 182, 183, 188, 207, 212 (bottom), 229, 231 (left); Wide World Photos, Inc., 152; David Williams, WNDU-TV, South Bend, Indiana, 55, 226 (lower right), 233, 234, 235; Courtesy of WMAQ-TV, NBC, Chicago, 121; James Sterne, 98, 99.

Loyola University Press is also grateful to the Chicago Daily News, WLS-AM, and WMAQ-TV for permission to photograph their offices, studios, and production facilities.